URBAN
TRAILS
OLYMPIA

URBAN TRAILS

TRAILS

OLYMPIA

South Sound Parks · Capitol State Forest
Shelton · Harstine Island

CRAIG ROMANO

MOUNTAINEERS
BOOKS

**MOUNTAINEERS
BOOKS**

Mountaineers Books is the publishing division of The Mountaineers, an organization founded in 1906 and dedicated to the exploration, preservation, and enjoyment of outdoor and wilderness areas.

1001 SW Klickitat Way, Suite 201, Seattle, WA 98134
800.553.4453, www.mountaineersbooks.org

Printed in China
Distributed in the United Kingdom by Cordee, www.cordee.co.uk
First edition: first printing 2017, third printing 2022

Copy editor: Emily Barnes
Design: Jen Grable
Layout: Peggy Egerdahl
Cartographer: Bart Wright, Lohnes+Wright
All photos by author unless noted otherwise.

Cover photograph: *Soak in the sight of the Deschutes River (Trail 3).*
Frontispiece: *A beautiful day for a run around Capitol Lake (Trail 1)*

Library of Congress Cataloging-in-Publication Data
Names: Romano, Craig, author.
Title: Urban trails. Olympia : South Sound Parks, Capitol State Forest, Shelton, Harstine Island / Craig Romano.
Description: Seattle, WA : Mountaineers Books, [2017] | Includes index.
Identifiers: LCCN 2017010038| ISBN 9781680510263 (ppb) | ISBN 9781680510270 (ebook)
Subjects: LCSH: Outdoor Recreation—Washington (State)—Olympia—Guidebooks.
  | Hiking—Washington (State)—Olympia—Guidebooks. | Trails—Washington (State)—Olympia—Guidebooks. | Olympia (Wash.)—Guidebooks. | Olympia (Wash.)—Tours.
Classification: LCC GV199.42.W22 O477 2017 | DDC 796.5109797/79—dc23
LC record available at https://lccn.loc.gov/2017010038

Mountaineers Books titles may be purchased for corporate, educational, or other promotional sales, and our authors are available for a wide range of events. For information on special discounts or booking an author, contact our customer service at 800-553-4453 or mbooks@mountaineersbooks.org.

ISBN (paperback): 978-1-68051-026-3
ISBN (ebook): 978-1-68051-027-0

CONTENTS

OLYMPIA METRO AREA

CAPITOL STATE FOREST

SOUTH THURSTON COUNTY

SHELTON

Hawthorns at Pioneer Park (Trail 4)

HARSTINE ISLAND

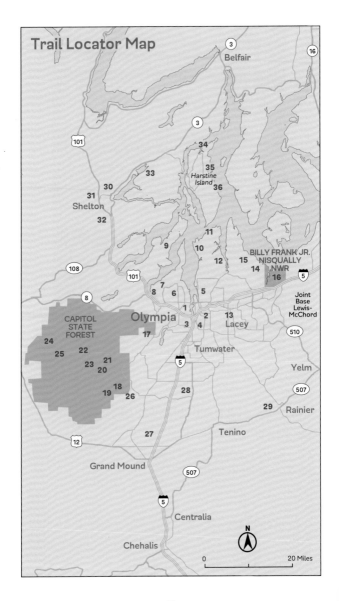

Trail Locator Map

TRAILS AT A GLANCE

Trail and/or Park	Distance	Walk	Hike	Run	Kids	Dogs
OLYMPIA METRO AREA						
1. Capitol Lake	4 miles of trails	•		•	•	•
2. Watershed Park	2.5 miles of trails		•	•		•
3. Tumwater Falls	1-mile loop	•			•	
4. Pioneer Park	2 miles of trails	•		•	•	•
5. Priest Point Park	more than 3 miles of trails		•		•	•
6. Grass Lake Nature Park	1.4 miles roundtrip	•	•		•	
7. Evergreen State College Beach	2 miles roundtrip		•		•	•
8. William Cannon Trail	1.5 miles roundtrip	•		•	•	
9. Frye Cove County Park	1.5 miles of trails	•		•	•	•
10. Burfoot County Park	1.5 miles of trails	•			•	•
11. Woodard Bay Natural Resources Conservation Area	3 miles of trails	•	•		•	
12. Chehalis Western Trail	up to 20.5 miles one-way	•		•	•	•
13. Woodland Creek Park and Woodland Trail	up to 5.2 miles one-way	•		•		•
14. William Ives Trail	2.6 miles roundtrip	•		•	•	•
15. Tolmie State Park	3 miles of trails	•	•	•	•	•
16. Billy Frank Jr. Nisqually National Wildlife Refuge	3 miles of trails	•	•		•	

Trail and/or Park	Distance	Walk	Hike	Run	Kids	Dogs
CAPITOL STATE FOREST						
17. McLane Creek	1.5 miles of trail	•	•		•	•
18. Mima Falls	6-mile loop		•	•	•	•
19. Bob Bammert Grove	1.1 miles roundtrip		•		•	•
20. Lost Valley Loop	8-mile loop		•	•	•	•
21. Little Larch Mountain	4 miles roundtrip		•		•	•
22. Capitol Peak	17-mile loop		•	•		•
23. Fuzzy Top	1.4 miles roundtrip		•		•	•
24. Porter Falls	1.6 miles roundtrip		•		•	•
25. Porter Trail	13 miles one-way		•	•	•	•
SOUTH THURSTON COUNTY						
26. Mima Mounds Natural Area Preserve	2.8 miles roundtrip	•	•		•	
27. Scatter Creek Wildlife Area	3.2 miles of trails	•	•		•	•
28. Millersylvania State Park	more than 8 miles of trails	•	•	•	•	•
29. Yelm–Tenino Trail	up to 14 miles one-way	•		•	•	•
SHELTON						
30. Huff N Puff Trail	1.85 miles of trails	•		•	•	•
31. Goldsborough Creek	1 mile roundtrip	•			•	•
32. Lake Isabella State Park	more than 4 miles of trails	•	•	•	•	•
33. Oakland Bay County Park	1.2 miles of trails	•	•		•	

Trail and/or Park	Distance	Walk	Hike	Run	Kids	Dogs
HARSTINE ISLAND						
34. Jarrell Cove State Park	1 mile of trails	•			•	•
35. Harstine Island State Park	3 miles of trails		•	•	•	•
36. Fudge Point State Park	3 miles roundtrip/0.6 mile of beach		•		•	•

INTRODUCTION
TRAILS FOR FUN AND FITNESS
IN YOUR BIG BACKYARD

LET'S FACE IT: WHETHER YOU'RE a hiker, walker, or runner, life can get in the way when it comes to putting time in on the trail. Far too often, it's hard for most of us to set aside an hour—never mind a day, or even longer—to hit the trails of our favorite parks and forests strewn across the state. But that doesn't mean we can't get out on the trail more frequently. Right in and near our own communities are thousands of acres of parks and nature preserves containing hundreds of miles of trails. And we can visit these pocket wildernesses, urban and urban-fringe parks and preserves, greenbelts, and trail corridors on a whim—for an hour or two without having to drive far. Some of these places we can even visit without driving at all—hopping on the bus instead—lessening our carbon footprint while giving us more time to relax from our hurried schedules.

Urban Trails: Olympia focuses on the myriad of trails, parks, and preserves within the urban, suburban, and rural-fringe areas around Olympia, Lacey, Tumwater, Shelton, and Harstine Island. You'll find trails to beaches, old-growth

Opposite: Billy Frank Jr. Nisqually National Wildlife Refuge's boardwalk (Trail 16) is a hit with young hikers.

Nonnative bullfrog at McLane Creek (Trail 17)

forests, lakeshores, riverfronts, shorelines, wildlife-rich wetlands, rolling hills, scenic vistas, meadows, historic sites, and vibrant communities. While often we equate hiking trails with the state's wildernesses and forests, there are plenty of accessible trails and areas of natural beauty in the midst of our population centers. The routes included here are designed to show you where you can go for a good run, long walk, or quick hike right in your own backyard.

This guide has two missions. One is to promote fitness and get you outside more often! A trip to Mount Rainier, North Cascades, or Olympic national parks can be a major undertaking for many of us. But a quick outdoor getaway to a local park or trail can be done almost anytime—before work, during a lunch break, after work, or when we don't feel like fighting traffic and driving for miles. And nearly all of these trails are available year-round; so you can walk, run, or hike every day by utilizing the trails within your own neighborhood. If you feel you are not getting outside enough or getting enough exercise, this book can help you achieve a healthier lifestyle.

Mission number two of this guide is to promote the local parks, preserves, and trails that exist within and near our urban areas. More than 4.7 million people (65 percent of Washington State's population) call the greater Puget Sound home. While conservationists continue to promote protection of our state's large, roadless wild corners—and that is still important—it's equally important that we promote the preservation of urban natural areas and develop more trails and greenbelts right where people live. Why? For one thing, the Puget Sound area contains unique and threatened ecosystems that deserve to be protected as much as those in wilder, more remote places. And we need to have usable and accessible trails where people live, work, and spend the majority of their time. Urban trails and parks allow folks to bond with nature and be outside on a regular basis. They help us cut our carbon footprint by giving us access to recreation without the need to burn excessive gallons of fuel to reach a destination. They make it easier for us to commit to regular exercise programs, giving us safe and agreeable places to walk, run, and hike. And urban trails and parks also allow disadvantaged populations—folks who may not have cars or the means to travel to one of our national parks or forests—a chance to experience nature and a healthy lifestyle too. As the greater Puget Sound area continues to grow in population and becomes increasingly more developed, it is all the more important that we support the expansion of our urban parks and trails.

So get out there, get fit, and have fun! And don't forget to advocate for more trails and parks.

HOW TO USE THIS GUIDE

THIS EASY-TO-USE GUIDE PROVIDES YOU with enough details to get out on the trail with confidence, while leaving enough room for your own personal discovery. I have walked, hiked, or run every mile of trail described here, and the directions and advice are accurate and up to date. Conditions can and do change, however, so make sure you check on the status of a park or trail before you go.

THE DESTINATIONS

This book includes thirty-six destinations, covering trails in and around Olympia, Shelton, and Harstine Island. Each one begins with the park or trail name followed by a block of information detailing the following:

Distance. Here you will find round-trip mileage (unless otherwise noted) if the route describes a single trail, or the total mileage of trails within the park, preserve, or greenway if the route gives an overview of the destination's trail system. Note that while I have measured most of the trails in this book with GPS and have consulted maps and governing land agencies, the distance stated may not always be exact—but it'll pretty darn close.

Elevation gain. For individual trails, elevation gain is for the *cumulative* difference on the route (and return), meaning not only the difference between the high and low points on the trail, but also for all other significant changes in elevation along the way. For destinations where multiple routes are given, as in a trail network within a park, the elevation gain applies to the steepest trail on the route.

High point. The high point is the highest elevation of the trail or trail system. Almost all of these trails are at a relatively low elevation, ensuring mostly snow-free access.

Difficulty. This factor is based not only on length and elevation gain of a trail or trails, but also on the type of tread and surface area of the trail(s). Most of the trails in this book are easy or moderate for the average hiker, walker, or runner. Depending on your level of fitness, you may find the trails more or less difficult than described.

Fitness. This description denotes whether the trail is best for hikers, walkers, or runners. Generally, paved trails will be of more interest to walkers and runners, while rough, hilly trails

A NOTE ABOUT SAFETY

Safety is an important concern in all outdoor activities. No guidebook can alert you to every hazard or anticipate the limitations of every reader. Therefore, the descriptions of roads, trails, routes, and natural features in this book are not representations that a particular place or excursion will be safe for your party. When you follow any of the routes described in this book, you assume responsibility for your own safety. Under normal conditions, such excursions require the usual attention to traffic, road and trail conditions, weather, terrain, the capabilities of your party, and other factors. Some of the lands in this book are subject to development or change of ownership. Always check current conditions and obey posted private property signs. Keeping informed on current conditions and exercising common sense are the keys to a safe, enjoyable outing.

—Mountaineers Books

will appeal more to hikers. Of course, you are free to hike, walk, or run (unless running is specifically prohibited) on any of the trails in this book.

Family-friendly. Here you'll find notes on a trail's or park's suitability for children and any cautions to be aware of, such as cliffs, heavy mountain-bike use, and so on. Some trails may be noted as suitable for jogger-strollers or as ADA-accessible.

Dog-friendly. This denotes whether dogs are allowed on the trail and what regulations (such as leashed or under voice control) apply.

Amenities. The featured park's amenities can include privies, drinking water, benches, interpretive signs and displays, shelters, learning centers, campgrounds, and dog-poop bag dispensers, to name a few.

Contact/maps. Here you'll find contact info for where to get current trail conditions. All websites and phone numbers for trail and park managers or governing agencies can be found in the Resources section at the end of the book. These websites will often direct you to trail and park maps; in some cases, a better or supplemental map is noted (such as Green Trails).

GPS. GPS coordinates in degrees and decimal minutes (based on the WGS84 datum) are provided for the main trailhead, to help get you to the trail.

Before You Go. This optional category notes any fees or permits required, hours the park or preserve is open (if limited), closures, and any other special concerns.

Next, I describe how to get to the trailhead via your own vehicle or by public transport if available.

GETTING THERE. Driving: This section provides directions to the trailhead—generally from the nearest large town or major road, and often from more than one direction—and also parking information. **Transit:** If the trailhead is served by public transportation, this identifies the bus agency and line.

EACH HIKE begins with an overview of the featured park or trail, highlighting its setting and character, with notes on the property's conservation history.

GET MOVING. This section describes the route or trails and what you might find on your hike, walk, or run, and may note additional highlights beyond the trail itself, such as points of historical interest.

GO FARTHER. Here you'll find suggestions for making your hike, walk, or run longer within the featured park—or perhaps by combining this trip with an adjacent park or trail.

PERMITS, REGULATIONS, AND PARK FEES

Many of the trails and parks described in this book are managed by county and city parks departments, requiring no permits or fees. Destinations managed by Washington State Parks and the Washington Department of Natural Resources (DNR) require a day-use fee in the form of the Discover Pass (www.discoverpass.wa.gov) for vehicle access. A Discover Pass

Conservation groups have been active preserving the South Sound's dwindling prairies.

costs $10 per vehicle per day or $30 for up to two vehicles annually. You can purchase the pass online, at many retail outlets, or better yet, from a state park office to avoid the $5 handling fee. Each hike in this book clearly states if a fee is charged or a pass is required.

Regulations, such as whether dogs are allowed or whether a park has restricted hours or is closed for certain occasions (such as during high fire danger or for wildlife management), are clearly spelled out in the trail information blocks.

ROAD AND TRAIL CONDITIONS

In general, trails change little year to year. But change can occur, and sometimes very quickly. A heavy storm can wash out sections of trail or access road in moments. Wind storms can blow down multiple trees across trails, making paths impassable. Lack of adequate funding is also responsible for trail neglect and degradation. For some of the wilder destinations in this book, it is wise to contact the appropriate land manager after a significant weather event to check on current trail and road conditions.

On the topic of trail conditions, it is vital that we acknowledge the thousands of volunteers who donate tens of thousands of hours to trail maintenance each year. The Washington Trails Association (WTA) alone coordinates more than 100,000 hours of volunteer trail maintenance each year. But there is always a need for more. Our trail system faces ever-increasing threats, including lack of adequate trail funding. Consider joining one or more of the trail and conservation groups listed in the Resources section.

OUTDOOR ETHICS

Strong, positive outdoor ethics include making sure you leave the trail (and park) in as good a condition as you found it—or even better. Get involved with groups and organizations that safeguard, watchdog, and advocate for land protection. And get on the phone and keyboard, and let land managers and public officials know how important protecting lands and trails is to you.

All of us who recreate in Washington's natural areas have a moral obligation and responsibility to respect and protect our natural heritage. Everything we do on the planet has an impact—and we should strive to have as little negative impact as possible. The **Leave No Trace Center for Outdoor Ethics** is an educational, nonpartisan, nonprofit organization that was developed for responsible enjoyment and active stewardship of the outdoors. Their program helps educate outdoor enthusiasts about their recreational impacts and recommends techniques to prevent and minimize such impacts. While geared toward backcountry use, many Leave No Trace (LNT) principles are also sound advice for urban and urban-fringe parks too, including planning ahead, disposing of waste properly, and being considerate of other visitors. To learn more, visit www.lnt.org.

TRAIL ETIQUETTE

We need to be sensitive not only to the environment surrounding our trails but to other trail users as well. Some of the trails in this book are also open to mountain bikers and equestrians. When you encounter other trail users, whether they are hikers, runners, bicyclists, or horseback riders, the only hard-and-fast rule is to follow common sense and exercise simple courtesy. With this Golden Rule of Trail Etiquette firmly in mind, here are other things you can do during trail encounters to make everyone's trip more enjoyable:

- Observe the right-of-way. When meeting bicyclists or horseback riders, those of us on foot should move off the trail. This is because hikers, walkers, and runners are more mobile and flexible than other users, making it easier for us to quickly step off the trail.
- Move aside for horses. When meeting horseback riders specifically, step off the downhill side of the trail unless the terrain makes this difficult or dangerous. In that case, move to the uphill side of the trail, but crouch down a bit so you do not tower over the horses' heads. Also, make yourself visible so as not to spook the big beastie, and talk in a normal voice to the riders. This calms the horses. If walking with a dog, keep your buddy under control.
- Stay on trails. Don't cut switchbacks, take shortcuts, or make new trails; all lead to erosion and unsightly trail degradation.
- Obey the rules specific to the trail or park you are visiting. Many trails are closed to certain types of use, including dogs and mountain bikes.
- Keep dogs under control. Trail users who bring dogs should have them on a leash or under very strict

voice-command at all times. And if leashes are required, then this does apply to you. Many trail users who have had negative encounters with dogs (actually with the dog owners) on the trail are not fond of, or are even afraid of, encountering dogs. Respect their right *not* to be approached by your darling pooch. A well-behaved, leashed dog, however, can certainly help warm up these folks to a canine encounter.

- **Avoid disturbing wildlife.** Observe from a distance, resisting the urge to move closer to wildlife (use your telephoto lens). This not only keeps you safer but also prevents the animal from having to exert itself unnecessarily to flee from you.
- **Take only photographs.** Leave all natural features and historic artifacts as you found them for others to enjoy.
- **Never roll rocks off trails or cliffs.** Gravity increases the impact of falling rocks exponentially, and you risk endangering lives below you.
- **Mind the music.** Not everyone (almost no one) wants to hear your blaring music. If you like listening to music while you run, hike, or walk, wear headphones and respect other trail users' right to peace and quiet—and to listening to nature's music.

HUNTING

Some of the destinations in this book (such as Capitol State Forest) are open to hunting. Season dates vary, but generally in Washington big-game hunting begins in early August and ends in late November. Also, bird hunting is popular in the outskirts (beyond trails) of the Billy Frank Jr. Nisqually National Wildlife Refuge during the winter months. While using trails in areas frequented by hunters, it is best to make yourself visible by donning an orange cap and vest. If hiking with a dog, your buddy should wear an orange vest too.

BEARS AND COUGARS

Washington harbors healthy populations of black bears, found in many of the parks and preserves along the urban fringe. If you encounter a bear while hiking, you'll usually just catch a glimpse of its bear behind. But occasionally the bruin may actually want to get a look at *you*.

To avoid an un-*bear*-able encounter, practice bear-aware prudence: Always keep a safe distance. Remain calm, do not look a bear in the eyes, speak in a low tone, and do not run from it. Hold your arms out to appear as big as possible. Slowly move away. The bear may bluff-charge—do not run. Usually the bear will leave once

Mossy black bear signpost in Priest Point Park (Trail 5)

he perceives he is not threatened. If he does attack, fight back using fists, rocks, trekking poles, or bear spray if you are carrying it.

Our state also supports a healthy population of *Felix concolor*. While cougar encounters are extremely rare, they do occur—even occasionally in parks and preserves on the urban fringe. Cougars are cats—they're curious. They may follow hikers, but rarely (almost never) attack adult humans. Minimize contact by not hiking or running alone and by avoiding carrion. If you do encounter a cougar, remember the big cat is looking for prey that can't or won't fight back. Do not run, as this may trigger its prey instinct. Stand up and face it. If you appear aggressive, the cougar will probably back down. Wave your arms, trekking poles, or a jacket over your head to appear bigger, and maintain eye contact. Pick up children and small dogs and back away slowly if you can do so safely, not taking your eyes off it. If it attacks, throw things at it. Shout loudly. If it gets close, whack it with your trekking pole, fighting back aggressively.

WATER AND GEAR

While most of the trails in this book can be enjoyed without much preparation or gear, it is always a good idea to bring water, even if you're just out for a quick walk or run. Even better, carry a small pack with water, a few snacks, sunglasses, and a rain jacket.

THE TEN ESSENTIALS

If you are heading out for a longer adventure—perhaps an all-day hike in the Capitol State Forest—consider packing the **Ten Essentials**, a list developed by The Mountaineers of items that are good to have on hand in an emergency:

- Navigation. Carry a map of the area you plan to be in and know how to read it. A cell phone or GPS unit are good to have along too.

- **Sun protection.** Even on wet days, carry sunscreen and sunglasses; you never know when the clouds will lift, and you can easily sunburn near water.
- **Insulation.** Storms can and do blow in rapidly. Carry rain gear, wind gear, and extra layers.
- **Illumination.** If caught out after dark, you'll be glad you have a headlamp or flashlight so that you can follow the trail home.
- **First-aid supplies.** At the very least, your kit should include bandages, gauze, scissors, tape, tweezers, pain relievers, antiseptics, and perhaps a small manual.
- **Fire.** While being forced to spend the night out is not likely on these trails, a campfire could provide welcome warmth in an emergency, with matches kept dry in a zip-lock bag.
- **Repair kit and tools.** A pocketknife or multitool can come in handy, as can basic repair items such as nylon cord, safety pins, a small roll of duct tape, and a small tube of superglue.
- **Nutrition.** Pack a handful of nuts or sports bars for emergency pick-me-ups.
- **Hydration.** Bring enough water to keep you hydrated, and for longer treks consider a means of water purification.
- **Emergency shelter.** It can be as simple as a plastic garbage bag, or a rain poncho that can double as an emergency tarp.

TRAILHEAD CONCERNS

By and large, our parks and trails are safe places. Common sense and vigilance, however, are still in order. This is true for all trail users, but particularly so for solo ones. Be aware of your surroundings at all times. Let someone know when and where you're headed out.

Sadly, car break-ins are a common occurrence at some of our parks and trailheads. Absolutely under no circumstances

Camas in bloom at Mima Mounds (Trail 26)

leave anything of value in your vehicle while out on the trail. Take your wallet and smartphone with you. A duffel bag on the backseat may contain dirty T-shirts, but a thief may think there's a laptop in it. Save yourself the hassle of returning to a busted window by not giving criminals a reason to clout your car.

If you arrive at a trailhead and someone looks suspicious, don't discount your intuition. If something doesn't feel right, it probably isn't. Take action by leaving the place or situation promptly. If the person behaves inappropriately or aggressively, take notes on his appearance and his vehicle's make and license plate, and report his behavior to the authorities. Do not confront the person; leave and go to another trail.

There's no need to be paranoid, though; our trails and parks are generally pretty safe. Just use a little common sense and vigilance while you're out and about.

Next page: *Beach at Burfoot County Park (Trail 10)*

OLYMPIA METRO AREA

Olympia sits on the shores of Budd Inlet, at the extreme southern end of Puget Sound. Home to eclectic Evergreen State College, this small state capital of 55,000 and neighboring Tumwater (population 25,000) are two of the oldest cities in the state. In 1845 a pioneer party arrived in Tumwater via the Cowlitz Trail from Fort Vancouver and established the first permanent non-Native settlement on Puget Sound. A year later Edmund Sylvester and Levi Smith jointly claimed land just to the north of Tumwater. Their claim was the beginning of Olympia, named for its view of the Olympic Mountains. Olympia became the territorial capital in 1853 and officially incorporated in 1859.

The city of Lacey (population 55,000), to the east of Olympia and Tumwater, was originally settled by pioneers as Woodland in 1853. It was incorporated in 1966 and has recently experienced explosive growth. Home to St. Martin's University, Lacey—like Olympia—supports a thriving educational and cultural scene and a large running community. Olympia held the first Women's Marathon Olympic Trials back in 1984. Today it is home to several running clubs and one of the state's best running specialty stores.

All three of these cities contain and are surrounded by an extensive park system—as well as a growing trail system. For runners, walkers, and hikers, the Olympia area offers miles of trails that hug the Puget Sound shoreline, wind through historic districts, and traverse pockets of mature forest and remnant prairies. And when the sun is shining, many of the region's parks and trails come with a knockout view of Mount Rainier or the craggy Olympic Mountains.

1 Capitol Lake

DISTANCE:	4 miles of trails
ELEVATION GAIN:	Up to 100 feet
HIGH POINT:	100 feet
DIFFICULTY:	Easy
FITNESS:	Walkers, runners
FAMILY-FRIENDLY:	Yes and stroller-friendly
DOG-FRIENDLY:	On-leash
AMENITIES:	Restrooms, water, benches, interpretive signs
CONTACT/MAPS:	Washington Department of Enterprise Services; map available online
GPS:	N 47° 02.232", W 122° 54.706"

GETTING THERE

Driving: From Lacey and points north, take Interstate 5 south to exit 103. Proceed 0.1 mile south on N. 2nd Avenue SW and turn left onto Custer Way SW. Continue 0.1 mile west and turn right onto Boston Street SW. After 0.1 mile turn right onto Deschutes Way SW (which becomes the Deschutes Parkway SW). Now drive north 0.3 mile to Tumwater Historical Park turnoff (Grant Street SW); 0.7 mile to Interpretive Park; or 1.6 miles to Marathon Park. Parking is also available along Deschutes Way SW. From Tumwater, take I-5 north to exit 103 and follow Deschutes Way SW north to parking and parks (described above).

Transit: Intercity Transit Routes 43 and 44 service the Marathon Park area and points north.

A former tidal basin transformed into an artificial lake, Capitol Lake beautifully reflects the domed state legislative building (state capitol) perched on a bluff above it. The civic pride of Washington's capital city, Capitol Lake is a hub of physical activity. Runners and walkers from near and far never take a rest from running alongside this nearly

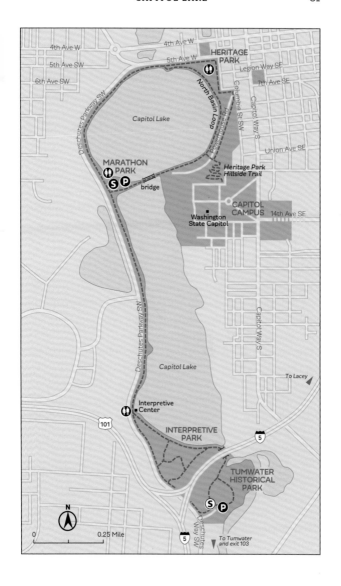

2-mile-long lake lined with parks and commemorative monuments.

GET MOVING

One of the most aesthetically appealing urban parks in Washington, Capitol Lake blends in beautifully among the surrounding city, sound, forests, and mountains. The lake is part of the greater Capitol Campus, which was designed adhering to principles of the City Beautiful Movement during the Progressive Era in the early twentieth century. This architectural plan emphasized beautification and monumental grandeur to enhance citizens' quality of life and to promote a harmonious social order. Most of the campus was designed by Walter Wilder and Harry White, who were influenced by the Olmsted brothers. The Capitol Campus was placed on the National Register of Historic Places in 1974.

If this is your first time visiting Capitol Lake—walk, don't run! You'll want to stop at all of the monuments and interpretive signs along the way and probably snap a few photos as well. The lake is graced with a greenbelt and traversed by concrete and soft-surface trails, allowing for several walking and running options. The most popular route—a 1.5-mile loop around the lake's North Basin—begins from Marathon Park.

Marathon Park commemorates the very first US trials for the Olympic Women's Marathon, held in 1984. It was here in Olympia that a young woman from Maine, Joan Benoit Samuelson, won the event (which started and finished from this spot) and secured her place at the Los Angeles Summer Olympic Games. She would then bring home a gold for America, winning the very first Olympic Women's Marathon event with a time of 2:24:52. For Joan and many other runners, Olympia is a special place.

From Marathon Park, run or walk the level 1.5-mile loop (crossing a narrow section of lake on a small bridge) around the North Basin through Heritage Park. About half the way is on soft surface, half on sidewalk. You'll pass a lot of monuments, attractive trees, and great views of the legislative building on a bluff above the lake. Want a close-up of the neoclassical domed building and a great workout to boot? Veer off the loop onto the 0.5-mile Heritage Park Hillside Trail and grind up a series of snaking switchbacks to Capitol Campus.

South of Marathon Park you can run or walk on sidewalk alongside the lake and Deschutes Parkway Southwest, reaching a small interpretive center in 0.8 mile. From here you can continue on sidewalk along Deschutes Way SW and climb a small hill to the entrance of Tumwater's Historical Park. Turn left and head downhill, passing some of the state's oldest homes and one of its oldest breweries, and reach a trail leading under I-5. Then take this paved trail along the lakeshore, returning to the interpretive center. This entire loop, from the interpretive center to Historical Park and back, is 1.2 miles. Add this loop to the North Basin loop, the out-and-back on the Heritage Park Hillside Trail, and an out-and-back on the connector stretch along the Deschutes Parkway, and you're looking at 5.3 miles.

2 Watershed Park

DISTANCE:	2.5 miles of trails
ELEVATION GAIN:	Up to 250 feet
HIGH POINT:	175 feet
DIFFICULTY:	Easy
FITNESS:	Hikers, runners
FAMILY-FRIENDLY:	Yes
DOG-FRIENDLY:	On-leash
AMENITIES:	Restrooms, interpretive signs, benches
CONTACT/MAPS:	Olympia Metropolitan Parks District; map available online
GPS:	N 47° 01.745", W 122° 53.367"

Boardwalk over Moxlie Creek

GETTING THERE

Driving: From downtown Olympia, follow 14th Avenue SE for 0.9 mile to a traffic circle at the junction with Henderson Boulevard SE. Proceed through the circle, exiting south on Henderson Boulevard SE (third exit). Then continue 0.1 mile to the G. Eldon Marshall trailhead and parking on your left.

From Lacey, follow Interstate 5 south to exit 105B. Then turn left onto Henderson Boulevard SE and continue 0.7 mile to the trailhead on your left. From Tumwater, follow I-5 north to exit 105 to 14th Avenue SE. Then immediately come to a traffic circle. Proceed through it, exiting south on Henderson Boulevard SE (third exit). Then continue 0.1 mile to the trailhead on your left.

Transit: Intercity Transit Route 94 services Watershed Park's pedestrian trailheads on Eastside Street SE and 22nd Avenue SE.

Wander through a lush, spring-fed ravine shaded by some of the biggest and oldest trees in Olympia. Marvel at the bubbling springs that once provided water for the capital

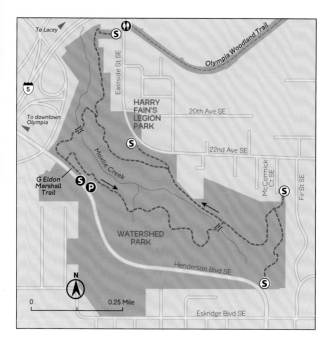

city. And locate remnants of old buildings and pipelines that once made up the city's waterworks. Now imagine that this 153-acre greenbelt (one of the city's most beloved parks) located just minutes from downtown Olympia was nearly clear-cut once municipal water operations ceased here. The park has a storied conservation history as well as a civic one. Enjoy learning about it as you hike its ravine-hugging, slope-plunging, basin-traversing trails.

GET MOVING

Five trailheads provide access to this park, but only the G. Eldon Marshall trailhead has parking. So don't be surprised if you encounter more folks on the trail than what the car tally in the lot would indicate. Watershed Park is quite popular with folks from adjoining neighborhoods.

Start your exploration on the G. Eldon Marshall Trail, named for a longtime civic leader once called "Mr. Olympia City Hall." World War II veteran Marshall was Olympia's city supervisor and manager for many years. Henderson Boulevard, a treed thoroughfare, was one of his favorite projects. Marshall passed away on Christmas Day in 2015.

In a couple hundred yards reach a junction. Here you can make a 1.4-mile loop of the park. If you go right, expect a few ups and downs—some via steps along the steep ravine walls surrounding the Moxlie Creek Springs Basin, one of the largest spring basins in the Puget Sound region. From the late 1800s until the 1950s, this basin provided Olympia with its water. The city then began using the McAllister Springs Basin for its water and slated a clear-cut of the old-growth in the Moxlie Creek Basin. What followed was a citizen protest, led by Margaret McKenny (see sidebar, "Citizen for the Future") and others, that went all the way to the state supreme court. The result? You're walking through it!

CITIZEN FOR THE FUTURE

An author, educator, conservationist, naturalist, and citizen activist, Margaret McKenny was responsible for saving and protecting some of Olympia's most prized parks and preserves. The daughter of a Civil War and Mexican War veteran who pioneered in Thurston County in 1867, McKenny was born in 1885. She attended the University of Washington and the Lowthorpe School of Landscape Architecture in Massachusetts. In 1919 she established a progressive kindergarten and primary school from her home in Olympia.

McKenny then spent several years on the East Coast before returning to Olympia in 1943. She would go on to create a nature radio program, and was the official photographer for the Washington State Parks Committee in 1945. In the 1950s she was active in civic groups whose mission was to beautify the area. Over the span of her life, she authored more than fifteen books, including working with famed ornithologist Roger Tory Peterson on several field guides. An expert on mushrooms and wildflowers, McKenny received several honors and awards for her writings.

McKenny was quite active in conservation issues and was responsible for the following successes: In the 1950s she was the founder of "Citizens for the Future," which was able to stop downtown's Sylvester Park from becoming a parking lot and prevented the cutting down of the oaks along Legion Way. In 1955 she led the group—ultimately taking its case all the way to the state supreme court—to protect what is now Watershed Park. She was instrumental in the movement to save the Nisqually Delta as well. McKenny passed away in 1969 at the age of eighty-four. An elementary school and a city park in Olympia, as well as a campground in the Capitol State Forest, have all been named in her honor.

Be sure to pause at all of the interpretive signs to read about this basin's history and the folks responsible for protecting it. The trail eventually crosses the creek via a boardwalk. The basin is thick with vegetation. Winter visits allow more creek views when foliage cover is sparse. In any season, be sure to stay on trails as the basin is a sensitive environment.

At 0.7 mile come to a junction. A trail leads right 0.5 mile, climbing steeply out of the basin and accessing trailheads on Henderson Boulevard Southeast and McCormick Court Southeast. The loop continues left, following alongside Moxlie Creek for a short way before climbing above it. At 0.9 mile reach another junction. The trail to the right continues climbing for about 0.15 mile, reaching a trailhead on 22nd Avenue Southeast.

The loop continues left, traversing a slope of big trees and reaching another junction at 1.2 miles. Here a trail heads right 0.35 mile to a trailhead on Eastside Street Southeast. The loop continues left, soon crossing Moxlie Creek and passing some remnants of the waterworks days. At 1.4 miles the trail returns to a familiar junction. The trailhead you started from is straight ahead a short distance.

GO FARTHER

Follow the trail leading to the Eastside Street Southeast trailhead. From there you can (carefully) cross Eastside Street Southeast and access the paved Olympia Woodland Trail (see Trail 13) for a much longer hike or run.

3	**Tumwater Falls**

DISTANCE:	1-mile loop
ELEVATION GAIN:	90 feet
HIGH POINT:	100 feet
DIFFICULTY:	Easy
FITNESS:	Walkers (running prohibited)
FAMILY-FRIENDLY:	Yes
DOG-FRIENDLY:	On-leash
AMENITIES:	Restrooms, interpretive signs, benches, gardens
CONTACT/MAPS:	Olympia Tumwater Foundation; map available online
GPS:	N 47° 00.830", W 122° 54.238"
BEFORE YOU GO:	Park open 8:00 AM until 30 minutes before sunset.

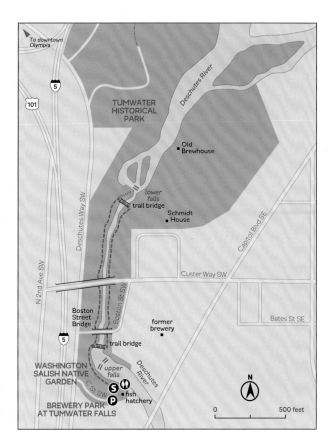

GETTING THERE

Driving: From Olympia, follow Interstate 5 south to exit 103. Continue a short distance south on N. 2nd Avenue SW and turn left onto Custer Way SW. Proceed east for 0.1 mile, crossing over the freeway and turning right onto Boston Street SW. Then drive 0.1 mile and turn left onto Deschutes Way SW. Continue for 0.2 mile and turn left onto C Street SW. Follow for 0.1 mile to Brewery Park at Tumwater Falls Park and trailhead.

The Deschutes River roars through Tumwater Falls Park.

Transit: Intercity Transit Route 13; Intercity Transit Route 12 services Custer Way SW; from there it's a 0.2-mile walk to the park.

Amble along manicured paths offering up-front, in-your-face views of a series of thundering falls famous for their beauty and their affiliation with beer. Walkers of all ages can saunter over footbridges and under historic road bridges to soak up a healthy dose of history along with sensational scenery.

GET MOVING

Owned and managed by the nonprofit Olympia Tumwater Foundation (OTF), Tumwater Falls is an iconic landmark in the South Sound. While the falls are well known to many area residents and visitors, the OTF is not as familiar. Created in 1950 by Olympia Brewing Company president Peter G. Schmidt (eldest son of brewery founder Leopold Schmidt), the OTF's mission is one of general philanthropy. OTF has supported medical research, historic preservation, education and scholarship programs, and the maintenance of both the historic Schmidt House and Brewery Park at Tumwater Falls.

The park was built on land donated by the Olympia Brewing Company (see sidebar, "It's the Water") and opened in 1962 (in anticipation that visitors to Seattle's World's Fair would make a stop here). It consists of 15 acres embracing the multitiered Tumwater Falls on the Deschutes River. With its meticulous gardens, stone walks, artificial feeder cascades, foot bridges, and ornamental trees, this park has a European flair.

From the parking area, follow a paved path past a salmon hatchery and enclosed fish ladder, immediately coming to the upper falls. The upper and lower falls are separated by a narrow gorge. Here the Deschutes River (named *Rivière des Chutes*, or River of the Falls, by early French-Canadian fur trappers) drops 82 feet into Capitol Lake on Eld Inlet. The name Tumwater is derived from the Chinook Jargon word for waterfall. *Tumtum*, another Chinook Jargon word, means "beating heart"—and as you walk along these pummeling and thundering waters, yours will probably race a little.

At the base of the upper falls, come to a junction. It matters not which way you go, as it's a loop. Go straight along the west bank of the river, or cross a bridge and continue hiking along the river's east bank. They meet up again at a replica of the famous bridge that once appeared on the labels of Olympia Beer, spanning the river above the lower falls. Both trails travel along the gorge between the upper and lower

IT'S THE WATER

Looming above thundering Tumwater Falls is a large, dormant brewery—perhaps once the most famous in the Pacific Northwest. Olympia Beer was brewed here for many decades, memorializing the lower falls and wooden bridge above them on millions of beer labels. The falls and the brewery were synonymous to many a Washingtonian, and when the brewery ceased operations, a part of Pacific Northwest history went flat.

Lured by the artesian well water near Tumwater Falls, German immigrant Leopold Friederich Schmidt opened the Capital Brewing Company here in 1896. In 1902, the brewery changed its name to the Olympia Brewing Company and launched its soon-to-be-famous slogan, "It's the water," to promote its flagship brew. Over the next many decades, those brews would be affectionately referred to as "Olys" by countless admirers.

In 1906, Schmidt moved his operation to a brick Mission Revival building at the base of the falls. However, ten years later, statewide Prohibition (predating national Prohibition) put a halt to beer making at the brewery. In 1934, a year after Prohibition was repealed, the company opened a newer and larger brewery at the base of the upper falls. The old brewery, a local landmark, still stands and is part of the Tumwater Historic District. In 1983, the Schmidt family sold the company to the Heileman Brewing Company. The brewery would be bought and sold a few more times before permanently closing in 2003—ending more than a century of beer making at the falls. Olympia Beer is still brewed by the Pabst Brewing Company—but it's not Washington water going into it these days; it's California water.

As you walk around the manicured grounds of Tumwater Falls, reflect on the area's brewing history. And perhaps finish your day with one of the fine microbrews currently being made in the region.

falls. Look down at the deep pools, eddies, and jumbled boulders. Look up at the historic 1915-built Boston Street Bridge spanning the gorge. And look all around at the lush vegetation surrounding you. In late spring, Washington's state flower, the Pacific rhododendron, adds some purples and pinks to the emerald band. Take time to read all of the informative panels on Tumwater—Washington's oldest permanent non-Native settlement on Puget Sound.

At the lower bridge walk the staircase (and be prepared to get wet) heading to the base of the lower falls. From here you look out across the southern end of Capitol Lake and see the original brewhouse. On your way back to the trailhead, be sure to check out the Washington Salish Native Garden (near the first pedestrian bridge). Here you can learn about native flora.

GO FARTHER

It's easy to combine a walk at Tumwater Falls with some of the parks at Capitol Lake (see Trail 1). Just walk about 0.3 mile north on sidewalks along Deschutes Way Southwest to the Tumwater Historical Park. From there you can continue on a paved trail to Olympia's Interpretive Park. It's also an easy walk via sidewalks along Boston Street, Custer Way, and Schmidt Place to the historic Schmidt House—the early twentieth-century home of the Olympia Brewing Company's founder and family.

4 Pioneer Park

DISTANCE:	2 miles of trails
ELEVATION GAIN:	None
HIGH POINT:	110 feet
DIFFICULTY:	Easy
FITNESS:	Walkers, runners
FAMILY-FRIENDLY:	Yes, paved trails ADA-accessible
DOG-FRIENDLY:	On-leash
AMENITIES:	Restrooms, water, benches, picnic tables, picnic shelter, playground, sports fields
CONTACT/MAPS:	City of Tumwater Parks and Recreation; no map online
GPS:	N 46° 59.769", W 122° 53.131"

GETTING THERE

Driving: From downtown Olympia, follow 14th Avenue SE for 0.9 mile to a traffic circle at the junction with Henderson Boulevard SE. Proceed through the circle, exiting south on Henderson Boulevard SE (third exit). Then continue south on Henderson Boulevard SE for 2.8 miles (passing the Yelm Highway intersection) to Pioneer Park, located on your right.

Alternatively, you can reach the park from Tumwater by following Custer Way east to Cleveland Avenue SE, which becomes Yelm Highway; then turn right (south) onto Henderson and follow to the park. The park can be reached from the south by following Tumwater Boulevard east to Henderson Boulevard SE; then turn left (north) and drive a short distance to the park.

Transit: Intercity Transit Route 68 stops at the intersection of Yelm Highway and Henderson Boulevard SE, where it's a pleasant, mostly downhill, 0.5-mile walk on sidewalk to the park.

Beyond this popular park's play equipment and manicured sports fields is a network of quiet trails along the Deschutes River and through an old orchard. Mosey down these paths, watching for birds and admiring some towering trees—including Oregon ashes. And when the sports fields are empty, the paved paths leading to them provide pleasant walking—and some good views too of the surrounding lush floodplain.

GET MOVING

Pioneer Park encompasses 85 acres of prime floodplain along the Deschutes River, not too far east from the river's famous falls. About half of the park has been converted to sports fields—the other half is in a seminatural state. You can access the park's trail system from several trailheads on the south side of the large and extended parking lot. On the east end,

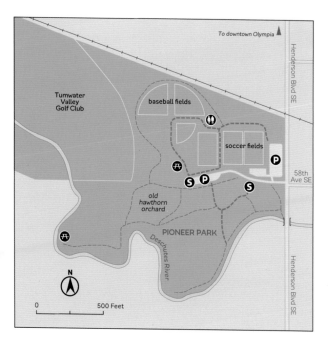

you can follow a 0.3-mile loop through some big trees with an extension to the Deschutes River.

This trail also accesses a wide path that follows along the river for about 0.4 mile, from the eastern end of the park near a road bridge to a big gravel bar at a bend in the river. Here the trail once went farther, but the river has changed its course over the years, washing away some tread. This spot now provides a good place for kids and dogs to splash about on a warm day. Always exercise caution, however, as currents can be swift and dangerous. The park has a kiosk with loaner life jackets for children.

At the west end of the paved loop, you can take several trails leading west across the floodplain. The trails are all

Deschutes River in Pioneer Park

short, usually just a quarter mile or so, but you can connect them and form loops and figure eights and get in a decent walk. Along the river, the vegetation is thick—composed of dogwoods and willows. The other trails traverse an old hawthorn orchard. Admire the hawthorn tree's blossoms in spring or its berries in fall. Birds are fond of the trees year-round.

At the far west end of the orchard, you can pick up a wide, rocky trail—part of the riverside trail that was severed by flooding years ago. Follow this quiet trail to a bend in the river, below a large bluff. Here is yet another spot your dog may be tempted to wet his paws. There are a couple of picnic tables here, making it a good spot to kick back and while away the day. I particularly love the large Oregon ash trees growing along the river here—pushing their northern limits.

When the sports fields are devoid of enthusiastic young athletes, consider walking the 0.7 mile of paved paths leading to and around them. You can also walk the perimeter of the soccer field and pick up a faint path—then a wide path— around the outer fields for another one-third mile of walking and running options. Here you'll also skirt the park's marshy northern grounds, which flourish with small mammals, amphibians, and birds.

If during your visit you see temporary arrows on the ground throughout the park, watch out for a wave of runners. The park is used by local high school cross-country teams to host meets. Cheer them on and then do your own run on the course.

5 Priest Point Park

DISTANCE:	More than 3 miles of trails
ELEVATION GAIN:	Up to 300 feet
HIGH POINT:	140 feet
DIFFICULTY:	Easy
FITNESS:	Hikers
FAMILY-FRIENDLY:	Yes
DOG-FRIENDLY:	On-leash
AMENITIES:	Restrooms, interpretive signs, benches, picnic tables and shelters
CONTACT/MAPS:	Olympia Metropolitan Parks District; map available online
GPS:	N 47° 04.273", W 122° 53.693"

GETTING THERE

Driving: From Lacey, follow Interstate 5 south to Olympia, taking exit 105B. (From Tumwater, follow I-5 north to Olympia, taking exit 105. Bear right at the fork, and turn right onto Henderson Boulevard SE. Then bear left onto Plum Street SE.)

Continue north on Plum Street for 0.6 mile to the junction with State Avenue NE. Then continue north, now on East Bay Drive NE, for 1.5 miles, turning right into Priest Point Park. Proceed 0.2 mile and turn left, crossing a bridge and reaching a parking lot and trailhead shortly afterward.

Much has changed on Budd Inlet since Father Pascal Ricard built his mission on Ellis Cove in 1848. The mission was short-lived, closing in 1860. But the city of Olympia, incorporated in 1859, thrived. Ironically, thanks to civic-minded folks in the early twentieth century, the area now named for Father Ricard—Priest Point—still bears semblance to the way it appeared in the 1800s. Now a 314-acre Olympia city park, Priest Point Park offers some of the best nature and beach walks within the city.

GET MOVING

There are several miles of trails within this park on Budd Inlet. Near the park's developed facilities on the east side of East Bay Drive Northeast are several short, interconnecting wooded trails. These make for good short walks, or perhaps a decent run if threaded together to create a series of loops. The park's supreme trail—and one of the nicest hikes in the South Sound—is Ellis Cove Trail. It's more or less a 2.2-mile lollipop loop with a couple of side trails if you're interested in extending it. This trail also offers a couple of access points to beaches on the inlet—allowing for extended roaming.

From the parking area west of the bridge, walk north on the park access road leading to East Bay Drive. At the road junction, note the trailhead kiosk. The way heads west into thick forest descending to the finger-of-an-inlet Ellis Cove. It then bends north to follow alongside the cove, dipping to cross a marshy section via a bridge and then climbing to higher land. The trail wraps around the cove and crosses Ellis Creek on a big boardwalk. It then comes to another

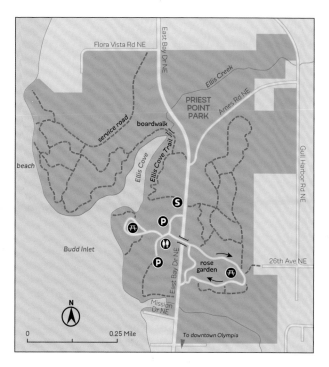

junction—this one marked with a mossy carved-bear sign. One of the nicest touches to this park is the wooded animal sculptures scattered about on trees and acting as signposts. When I first hiked here in the early 1990s, they were pretty fresh. Now they are well weathered and covered in mosses. It would be nice to have them restored, but even in their current condition, kids will love them.

The Ellis Cove Trail makes a loop at this junction. Go left or right. The way left travels along Ellis Cove and Budd Inlet, going up and over some ledges and bluffs. You'll pass some nice big madronas along the way. You'll also pass three beach access spurs. When the tide is low, plan on spending some time walking the broad, gravelly beach. Enjoy some good

Beach on Budd Inlet

views too of Olympia to the south. The trail then bends east-ward and climbs a forested bluff before descending back to the bear junction. If you want to explore even more terrain, there are two short connector trails on the loop allowing you to do a little forest walking on the bluff.

As you explore this thickly forested bluff and undeveloped coastline just north of Olympia's bustling port, try to pic-ture this place more than 150 years ago. Father Ricard and three other Catholic priests arrived from France and built the St. Joseph's Mission here to proselytize to local Native Americans. The mission consisted of a large garden, chapel, and school for boys from area tribes. It was short-lived but nevertheless had an impact on the area. In the 1930s, the park was a temporary camp for thousands of unemployed men who came to Olympia to protest. There's so much more to so many of our parks than the manicured trails that now traverse them.

6 Grass Lake Nature Park

DISTANCE:	1.4 miles roundtrip
ELEVATION GAIN:	up to 40 feet
HIGH POINT:	190 feet
DIFFICULTY:	Easy
FITNESS:	Walkers, hikers
FAMILY-FRIENDLY:	Yes
DOG-FRIENDLY:	Dogs prohibited
AMENITIES:	None
CONTACT/MAPS:	Olympia Metropolitan Parks District; map available online
GPS:	N 47° 04.273", W 122° 53.693"

GETTING THERE

Driving: From Lacey and Tumwater, follow Interstate 5 to US Highway 101 north and take the Evergreen Parkway exit. Then immediately exit onto Mud Bay Road NW (Business US 101) and turn right. Proceed for 0.5 mile and turn left onto Kaiser Road NW. (From downtown Olympia, head west on Harrison Avenue NW [Business US 101] and turn right onto Kaiser Road.) Now drive north for 0.4 mile to a small parking area on your right.

As its name denotes, **Grass Lake** is more of a marsh. And marshes teem with life. Take a walk here in the spring and be serenaded by a chorus line of woodland birds. Waterfowl congregate at the shrub-, reed-, sage-, and grass-filled lake. Small mammals live here too—watch for otters and beavers. Protecting the headwaters of Green Cove Creek, this 172-acre park is a pure delight for nature lovers. And Grass Lake is one of Olympia's least-crowded parks.

GET MOVING

From the small trailhead, walk across a manicured lawn, passing a city of Olympia municipal well. Locate a small kiosk and trail at the eastern end of the lawn. Entering a forest of alders, maples, and Douglas firs, follow a near-level, well-maintained path. At 0.3 mile reach an unmarked junction. Here, an old woods road leaves left, reaching Lake Louise within a couple

Salal forms a thick forest understory at Grass Lake Nature Park.

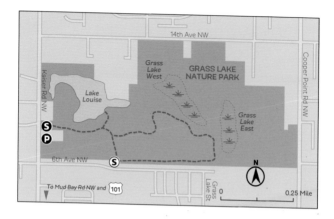

hundred feet. Unlike Grass Lake, Lake Louise looks like a lake. Scan the open waters for wildlife.

The main trail continues east, coming to a junction. It's a loop. If you head right, you'll climb a little and then bend left. Here a short trail leads right to a neighborhood trailhead on 6th Avenue Northwest. The main trail skirts a housing development before bending left near Grass Lake, which is actually two small marshy bodies of water—Grass Lake West and Grass Lake East. The brush is thick along the trail (especially the salal), granting extremely limited views of the lakes. This is a wildlife preserve—so stay on the trail and use a set of binoculars to search through the trees for any wildlife in the open wetlands. More than one hundred bird species and two hundred plant species have been recorded at this urban greenbelt. What will you see?

GO FARTHER

Not far from Grass Lake is Yauger Park (access from Cooper Point Road Northwest). It's a fairly developed park with sports facilities, but it has some nice walking paths and a track for running.

7

Evergreen State College Beach

DISTANCE:	2 miles roundtrip
ELEVATION GAIN:	110 feet
HIGH POINT:	110 feet
DIFFICULTY:	Easy
FITNESS:	Hikers
FAMILY-FRIENDLY:	Yes
DOG-FRIENDLY:	Yes
AMENITIES:	None
CONTACT/MAPS:	Evergreen State College; map available online
GPS:	N 47° 04.651", W 122° 58.346"
BEFORE YOU GO:	$2 parking fee on weekdays (pay at college visitors entrance station); no charge on weekends

GETTING THERE

Driving: From Lacey and Tumwater, follow Interstate 5 to US Highway 101 north for 3 miles and take the Evergreen Parkway exit. (From downtown Olympia, head west on Harrison Avenue NW to Evergreen Parkway NW). Then continue 2.2 miles to a roundabout. If it's a weekday, turn left here onto McCann Plaza Drive NW and proceed a short distance to the visitors center entrance station to purchase a parking permit. Then return to the roundabout and continue left on Evergreen Parkway for 0.2 mile, turning left onto Overhulse Place. Drive 0.5 mile and turn left onto Driftwood Road. Then proceed 0.4 mile to Parking Lot F. The trailhead is located on the north end of the lot.

Transit: Intercity Transit Route 41

The buildings of Evergreen State College, which was established in the 1960s, lack the classical and gothic architecture that grace many a college campus. But how many of those colleges and universities can lay claim to hundreds of acres of forest, a remote undeveloped beach, and miles of trails?

Evergreen can—and it fits nicely with the college's crunchy reputation. Enjoy roaming miles of trails on this 1000-plus-acre campus just a few miles west of downtown Olympia.

GET MOVING

Even if you study the map at the trailhead, you'll still be confused once you get moving. This is Evergreen State College—a nontraditional place—so don't expect any signs or trail markers along the way. It can be confusing on your first visit, and you may make a few unintentional turns. Of course, that can be half the fun. This book should help you find your way to the beach and back. You're free to check out all those radiating trails at will.

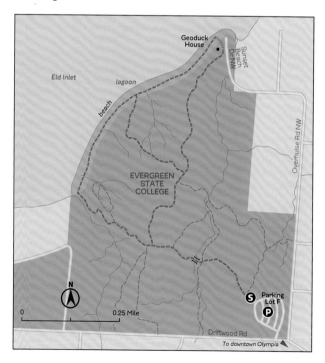

A hiker enjoys a quiet moment on Evergreen State College Beach.

On a wide and beaten path immediately enter a thick second-growth forest. Ignore side paths and follow the main path, slowly descending. Pass big cedars and big evergreen huckleberry bushes. After crossing a boardwalk, cross a small creek via a bridge. This spot is a favorite with *Greeners* (Evergreen students). Actually, the entire trail system and beach are popular with students and faculty, so expect to encounter some interesting folks along the way. The beach and forest are used for scientific study as well as recreation.

At 0.3 mile come to a Y junction. The trail left steeply drops and soon becomes rougher. At a muddy creek crossing, you can hike right to a bluff with limited views out to Eld Inlet, or you can hike left, following the creek and reaching the beach in about a quarter mile. The easier way to the beach continues right. Take it, coming to another junction at 0.5 mile. From this point you can make a nice loop that involves walking the beach (when the tide is low).

The trail right continues along a bluff, descending to the college's Geoduck House on Sunset Beach Drive Northwest (within the campus). If you choose to go this direction, ignore all trails leading left and reach the road after 0.4 mile. It's then a short walk left to the beach. If you choose to head left instead, steeply descend, reaching the beach near a lagoon in 0.3 mile. Now explore more than 0.6 mile of secluded sandy and cobbled beach on Eld Inlet. To make the suggested loop, hike 0.3 mile east to the beach's end at Bushoowah-Ahlee Point near Snyder Cove. Here take stairs to Sunset Beach Drive and walk a short distance to the Geoduck House. Then locate the return trail (on the east side of the house) and head back to the parking lot.

Feel free to explore 0.3 mile of beach west of the lagoon as well. You can also return to your start by following a trail (picked up near a creek) at the western end of the Evergreen Beach property. No matter your route, be sure to take your time on the beach and watch for a myriad of birds, mammals, and a few eclectic souls as well.

8 William Cannon Trail

DISTANCE:	1.5 miles roundtrip
ELEVATION GAIN:	None
HIGH POINT:	20 feet
DIFFICULTY:	Easy
FITNESS:	Walkers, runners
FAMILY-FRIENDLY:	Yes and stroller-friendly
DOG-FRIENDLY:	On-leash
AMENITIES:	Interpretive signs
CONTACT/MAPS:	Washington Department of Transportation; no map available online
GPS:	N 47° 03.000", W 122° 59.864"

GETTING THERE

Driving: From exit 104 on Interstate 5 in Olympia, head north on US Highway 101 for 4.6 miles, taking the 2nd Avenue and

Mud Bay Road exit. Turn right onto Mud Bay Road, and then immediately turn left onto Madrona Beach Road NW. Continue 0.3 mile to the Park and Ride. Park here—the trailhead is located at the northeast corner of the parking lot.

Transit: Mason County Transit Route 6, Olympia to Shelton

An inconspicuous trail tucked behind businesses and just a stone's throw away from busy US 101, the William Cannon Trail holds a few surprises. Take this level path along appropriately named Mud Bay and stand in wonderment at the natural world just beyond the buzz of vehicles and busy commercial structures. Look for eagles, herons, sandpipers, kingfishers, dabblers, divers, waders, and maybe an otter or two. The trail is short—but you'll want to

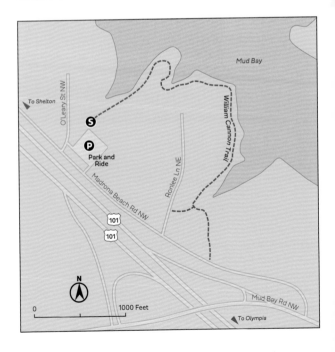

Trestle remnants of the Mud Bay Logging Company's rail line

spend time reading the historic panels and gazing out at the rich tidal mudflats.

GET MOVING

Also referred to as the Mud Bay Trail, this short trail isn't known to very many walkers. It was constructed in 2002 as a collaborative project involving several private businesses and public agencies: Duke Energy Company, Port of Olympia, Washington Department of Transportation, and the McLane School among them. The trail is named for William Cannon, one of the first non–Native Americans to see Puget Sound. Cannon was part of a multiethnic group of Hudson's Bay Company employees who passed through this area in 1824 on their way from Astoria on the Columbia River to Fort Langley on the Fraser River.

Now start walking and see the bay on Eld Inlet, one of the southernmost reaches of Puget Sound. The way is perfectly level, following a small cove while skirting businesses. Be sure to read the panels describing the area's logging and fishing history as well as its first peoples. Mud Bay is within the traditional lands of the Squaxins. It was a Squaxin, John Slocum, who founded the Indian Shaker Church in 1882, which combines elements of Catholicism, charismatic Protestantism, and traditional Native beliefs. The first Indian Shaker Church is located just to the west. Services are still being held there.

Come to a small point with a big Douglas fir. Check out (but don't venture upon) the extensive mudflats of Mud Bay. They are most impressive in low tides and this is when wildlife is most active—scavenging the flats for tasty morsels. Look north at the rows of pilings that once made up a railroad trestle for the Mud Bay Logging Company. Look too across the bay at forested shores not dissimilar to the ones Cannon saw—and ones quite a contrast from the one you are standing upon. A Squaxin village once sat directly across the bay.

Continue walking along the bay, catching views of the productive waterway through gaps in the Nootka rosebushes lining the path. The trail eventually scoots alongside another small cove before terminating on Madrona Beach Road Northwest. Now turn around and retrace your steps, looking for more wildlife and reflecting upon the fascinating history of this small parcel, which thousands of zooming motorists pass each day.

9   Frye Cove County Park

DISTANCE:	1.5 miles of trails
ELEVATION GAIN:	Up to 250 feet
HIGH POINT:	135 feet
DIFFICULTY:	Easy to moderate
FITNESS:	Walkers, runners
FAMILY-FRIENDLY:	Yes
DOG-FRIENDLY:	On-leash

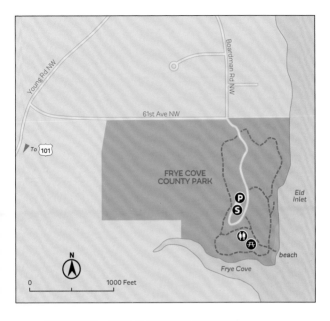

AMENITIES: Picnic shelter, privies, playground
CONTACT/MAPS: Thurston County Parks; no map available online
GPS: N 47° 06.991", W 122° 57.962"

GETTING THERE

Driving: From Olympia, head north on US Highway 101 (bearing right [north] at junction with State Route 8 at 5.7 miles) for 7.3 miles to Steamboat Island Road exit. Turn left onto Sexton Drive NW and proceed 0.3 mile, turning right onto Steamboat Island Road NW. In about a mile, turn right on Gravelly Beach Road NW, which becomes Gravelly Beach Loop NW in about 2 miles. After a sharp bend in the road, turn left onto Young Road NW. After 0.5 mile, turn right onto 61st Avenue NW. Continue east on 61st Avenue NW, bearing right at the intersection with Boardman Road NW and entering Frye Cove County Park in 0.5 mile. Proceed another 0.4 mile to parking and the trailhead.

Steps help hikers negotiate the ravines of Frye Cove County Park.

A small park tucked along a quiet cove on one of the long finger peninsulas that jut north into the South Puget Sound, Frye Cove offers some exceptional walking. The trail system is short, but the varied terrain includes ravines, a bluff, and a pretty beach with a knockout view of Mount Rainier. Locals come here to walk their dogs or work on their daily step counts. But for the most part, Frye Cove remains off the beaten path.

GET MOVING

Frye Cove County Park is only 67 acres in size, but it'll feel bigger if you meander on all the trails and perhaps (if the tide is low) partake in a little beach walking too. From the parking area, the main loop trail can easily be accessed. You can also reach the trail from within the heart of the park by walking the gated paved access road to the southeast of the parking lot.

Walk this 0.1-mile road—steeply descending through a big, treed ravine—and reach a grassy bluff complete with restroom facilities and sheltered picnic tables. The bluff overlooks Eld Inlet. And when the sky is clear, there's big, beautiful Mount Rainier looking right at you. You can quickly see why people have hosted reunions, get-togethers, and weddings here.

You can walk down to the rocky shore—and when the tide is low, feel free to wander on 1400 feet of beach. Frye Cove is to the right and it can get a little muddy—so you may want to instead observe it from the trail above. You can make a great little 1-mile loop here by going either left or right, following trails that run along the park's periphery. There are a couple of other shorter trails branching off from the loop—one heading to a viewpoint of Rainier, another offering a connector from the parking lot to the picnic area. Incorporate these into your walk—and perhaps backtrack a bit here and there—and you can easily double your mileage.

One thing is for certain—no matter the distance you choose to run or walk, you should get a decent workout in this little park. The trails go up and down, darting into and out of lush ravines. Steps along the way will help your ascents and descents and a couple of bridges should help keep your boots dry at creek crossings. Be sure to admire the trees within the park. There are some pretty large Douglas firs and bigleaf maples growing in the ravines. At the picnic area, you may have noticed an interesting hardwood species. These black locust trees, often grown to prevent soil erosion, are native to the eastern United States. The original homesteader who settled here probably came from back east and planted them. Their wood is used for fence posts, lumber, boxes, and many other uses. And bees are particularly fond of the black locust's nectar-rich blossoms, making this tree valuable for beekeeping.

10 Burfoot County Park

DISTANCE:	1.5 miles of trails
ELEVATION GAIN:	Up to 300 feet
HIGH POINT:	120 feet
DIFFICULTY:	Easy
FITNESS:	Walkers
FAMILY-FRIENDLY:	Yes
DOG-FRIENDLY:	On-leash
AMENITIES:	Restrooms, interpretive signs, playground, bike racks, benches, picnic tables and shelters
CONTACT/MAPS:	Thurston County Parks and Recreation; no map online
GPS:	N 47° 07.924", W 122° 54.083"

GETTING THERE

Driving: From Lacey, follow Interstate 5 south to Olympia, taking exit 105B. (From Tumwater, follow I-5 north to Olympia, taking exit 105. Bear right at the fork and turn right onto Henderson Boulevard SE. Then bear left onto Plum Street SE.) Continue north on Plum Street for 0.6 mile to a junction with State Avenue NE. Then continue north, now on East Bay Drive NE, for 2.2 miles through Priest Point Park. Stay on this road as it becomes Boston Harbor Road NE and drive north for 4.4 miles, turning left into Burfoot County Park to reach the trailheads.

Situated at the mouth of Budd Inlet, this little park packs in a lot of exploring opportunities. Take to its trails and discover deep ravines, towering trees, rugged bluffs, a quiet lagoon, and an inviting beach where you can take in views of the Olympic Mountains and enjoy sublime sunsets. Not bad when you consider Burfoot County Park is a mere 50 acres in size.

Boardwalk to the beach

GET MOVING

The park is compact but will feel much larger once you hit its trails. From the park road that loops around a field with picnic shelters, find a handful of trailheads. The trails on the park's western end drop into lush ravines shaded by big maples, grand firs, and a handful of other species. On the negative side, invasive holly has a firm grip here. On the positive side, native Pacific rhododendrons—Washington's state flower—can be found growing in the ravines and on the bluffs. Plan a visit in late spring to relish in their radiant beauty.

The beach can be reached a mere 0.25 mile from the two beach access trails. They both meet up in a ravine where a small creek drains into a lagoon. Walk across a boardwalk and reach the beach beneath some rocky bluffs. When the tide is low, you can walk north around the bluff to a grassy bench.

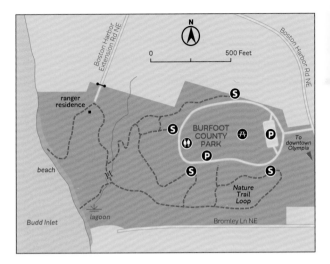

Here a paved road trail leads steeply uphill, passing the park's ranger residence and leading to a neighborhood (no public parking). Just north of the residence, a trail heads east—plummeting with the help of some stairs into a creek-cradling ravine and connecting to the beach trail. Park officials are planning on soon removing the road trail and doing some rehabilitation work around the bulkhead at the grassy bench. Expect some area closures and changes.

At the park's east end, several trails lead to paths traversing the bluff above the ravines. They make for easier walks since you can skip the steep descents and ascents to the beach. In the park's southeast corner, you can mosey on a nature trail loop. The loop is graced with weathered interpretive signs that include text in braille. To get a good workout at this small park, walk its periphery, utilizing the bluff trails and connecting them with a short jaunt on the park road. Then make a figure eight or two, down to the beach and back. You can get 2 miles under your belt this way—do it twice and you earned that morning muffin.

11 Woodard Bay
Natural Resources Conservation Area

DISTANCE:	3 miles of trails
ELEVATION GAIN:	Up to 250 feet
HIGH POINT:	100 feet
DIFFICULTY:	Easy
FITNESS:	Walkers, hikers
FAMILY-FRIENDLY:	Yes and some trails ADA-accessible
DOG-FRIENDLY:	Dogs prohibited
AMENITIES:	Privies, bike racks, interpretive signs, benches, picnic tables and shelters
CONTACT/MAPS:	Washington DNR, Southwest Puget Sound Regional Office; no map online
GPS:	N 47° 07.626", W 122° 51.209"
BEFORE YOU GO:	Discover Pass required
NOTE:	Vehicles are frequently broken into here. Do not leave valuables in your car, and report all suspicious activities to the authorities.

GETTING THERE

Driving: From Olympia, follow 4th Avenue East to a junction with Plum Street SE. Turn left (north) and drive (road becomes East Bay Drive NE) for 2.2 miles through Priest Point Park. Road then becomes Boston Harbor Road NE. Stay on this road and continue north for 2.9 miles, bearing right onto Woodard Bay Road NE. Follow for 1.6 miles to the main Woodard Bay trailhead on your left. (At 1.1 miles, the road bears left onto Libby Road NE. Immediately afterward, turn right back onto Woodard Bay Road NE.) The Overlook trailhead is reached by continuing on Woodard Bay Road NE another 0.2 mile to the Chehalis Western trailhead.

From Lacey (exit 108 on Interstate 5), drive north on Sleater-Kinney Road NE for 4.5 miles, bearing left onto 56th Avenue NE. Continue 0.4 mile and turn right onto Shincke

Road NE. Then proceed north 0.6 mile and turn left onto Woodard Bay Road NE. Drive 0.4 mile for Overlook Trail at the Chehalis Western trailhead on your right, or 0.6 mile to the main Woodard Bay trailhead on your right.

An 870-acre historical, cultural, and natural preserve just a few miles north of Olympia, Woodard Bay offers some of the area's most scenic and interesting trails. Woodard Bay protects more than five miles of Puget Sound shoreline. Wildlife is prolific here and chances are great of seeing seals, eagles, bats, guillemots, and herons. The conservation area's trails wind through mature forests, hug bay shorelines, and will take you to a small peninsula that served for more than fifty years as a busy railroad log dump.

GET MOVING

Woodard Bay was designated a Natural Resources Conservation Area (NRCA) in 1987—one of the first in the state. An area of relatively undisturbed shorelines, mature second-growth, and outstanding wildlife habitat, the region was once owned by Weyerhaeuser and boasted a rail line and a busy log dump. For fifty-six years, three to four trains of fifty to sixty cars dumped logs into Henderson Bay every day where they were rafted to a mill in Everett.

Today the area is managed as a natural and historical preserve. Besides retaining relics and structures from its industrial past, Woodard Bay protects some important wildlife habitat. The remaining section of the railroad log dump trestle acts as a spring and summer nursery for thousands of bats, and the preserve is home to a large heron and cormorant rookery. Bald eagles, pigeon guillemots, and purple martins all nest here. River otters and a large harbor seal population also inhabit the preserve. Woodard Bay houses an interpretive center used for environmental education. Don't be surprised if you run into a school group while you are out here exploring.

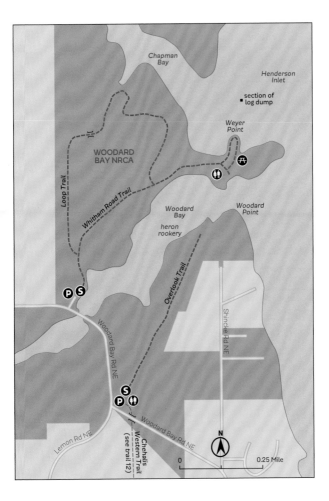

There are three main trails within the preserve. Two begin at the main parking area and can easily be combined. The other one begins from the Chehalis Western Trail's northern terminus, located 0.2 mile south of the main parking area.

Weyer Point

WHITHAM ROAD TRAIL

From the main parking area, follow this paved road (now turned nonmotorized trail) east to Weyer Point. This is the old access road to the log dump. Today it is a pleasant walk that almost anyone can make—young and old alike. It is also wheelchair accessible, but there is a small hill where some may need assistance.

The trail soon turns away from the bay and comes to a junction with the Loop Trail at 0.1 mile. The Whitham Road Trail continues right, climbing about fifty feet up a hillside sporting impressive bigleaf maples and grand firs. The way then descends, passing a view of Woodard Bay to the south. At 0.5 mile, come to the other end of the Loop Trail. Continue straight, reaching Weyer Point at 0.8 mile.

Plan on spending some time here: a kiosk, numerous interpretive panels, picnic tables, benches, a replica First Nations canoe, a restored boom foreman's office, and more points of interest can be found. A small loop trail circles this point, where the rail line once crossed Woodard Bay to the south and terminated at a long log dump extending north into Henderson Inlet at the mouth of Chapman Bay. A section of the log dump remains (but is not accessible to visitors), now acting as a bat nursery. Scan the old log booms for basking harbor seals.

Government agencies, in partnership with several conservation groups, have been busy removing creosote from the remaining structures as well as restoring some of the tidelands for Olympia oysters. After spending some time here learning about the region's history and watching for wildlife, either return the way you came or take the Loop Trail back.

LOOP TRAIL

Since this trail makes for a great return from Weyer Point, it is described here counterclockwise. The trail's eastern end can be reached 0.5 mile from the trailhead, or 0.3 mile from Weyer Point. Follow the single-track, soft-surface trail up a hill, climbing about sixty feet. Pass a pond made during a past logging operation—now supporting a healthy population of newts. Interpretive signs here give more insight.

The trail climbs and dips a bit, passing through a forest of big trees lining Chapman Bay. At about 0.4 mile, come to a bench in a cedar grove with a good view of Chapman Bay. The way then bends southwest and crosses a wetland via a long boardwalk. More ups and downs and another long boardwalk await you as you hike farther. After topping a 100-foot high point, the trail descends with the help of some stairs. At 1.2 miles reach the Whitham Road Trail. Turn right and walk 0.1 mile west to return to the trailhead.

OVERLOOK TRAIL

Note: The trail is closed from mid-March to August 15 to protect nesting herons. This trail starts from the northern terminus of the Chehalis Western Trail, a rail-trail that utilizes the bed of the original logging railroad that led from Weyerhaeuser tree farms to the log dump on Weyer Point.

The Overlook Trail is actually part of the original rail line as well. Follow this wide, smooth-graveled, ADA-accessible path northeast, gradually descending fifty feet or so. Pass benches and interpretive panels as you travel beneath a canopy of big mossy maples.

At 0.5 mile reach an overgrown overlook of Woodard Bay. Here a trestle once spanned the bay. The real interest now is the large heron and cormorant rookery—one of the largest in Puget Sound. Look up at the crowns of the towering cottonwoods to sight the nests and large birds perched upon them. In early spring, before the leaves have filled in the crowns, the nests and birds are easy to spot. Do your best to remain quiet and not disturb the nesting birds. Return the way you came.

12 Chehalis Western Trail

DISTANCE:	Up to 20.5 miles one-way
ELEVATION GAIN:	Up to 300 feet
HIGH POINT:	350 feet
DIFFICULTY:	Easy
FITNESS:	Walkers, runners
FAMILY-FRIENDLY:	Yes and stroller-friendly, but be aware of bicycles
DOG-FRIENDLY:	On-leash
AMENITIES:	Interpretive signs, restrooms, benches
CONTACT/MAPS:	Thurston County Parks; map available online
GPS:	N 47° 07.435", W 122° 51.015"

GETTING THERE

Driving: There are several trailheads and access points along this trail. Parking can be found at the following major trailheads:

Woodard Bay Road trailhead: From Olympia, follow 4th Avenue East to a junction with Plum Street SE. Turn left (north) and drive (road becomes East Bay Drive NE) for 2.2 miles through Priest Point Park. Road then becomes Boston

Harbor Road NE. Stay on this road and continue north for 2.9 miles, bearing right onto Woodard Bay Road NE. Follow this road for 1.8 miles to the trailhead on your left.

South Bay Road trailhead: From Olympia, follow 4th Avenue East for 1.3 miles, turning left onto Phoenix Street NE. Continue for 0.1 mile and turn right onto South Bay Road NE. Then proceed for 2.7 miles to the trailhead.

Chambers Lake trailhead: From Olympia, follow Interstate 5 north to exit 108A (from Lacey, take exit 108) and drive 0.8 mile south on Sleater-Kinney Road NE. Then turn right onto 14th Avenue SE and continue 0.3 mile to the trailhead on your left.

67th Avenue trailhead: From Lacey, head south on College Street SE for 3.4 miles to a junction with Yelm Highway. Then continue straight, now on Rainier Rd SE. After 0.6 mile, turn right onto a roundabout exiting onto 67th Avenue SE. Proceed 0.25 mile to the trailhead.

Fir Tree Road trailhead: From Tumwater, head north on Capitol Boulevard SE, turning right onto Custer Way SW. After 0.1 mile, turn right onto Cleveland Avenue SE, which becomes Yelm Highway, and continue for 2.8 miles. Then turn right onto Rich Road SE and drive 2.8 miles. Next, turn left onto Fir Tree Road SE and continue 2 miles to the trailhead on your left.

Transit: The Chehalis Western Trail can be accessed near Pacific Avenue SE via Intercity Routes 62B, 64, and 67. The Chambers Lake trailhead is serviced by Intercity Route 64. The 67th Avenue trailhead can be reached via a short walk after taking Intercity Route 64.

You can run or walk part or all 20.5 miles of this paved trail through the heart of Thurston County. From Woodard Bay on Henderson Inlet, this former logging railroad travels through forests, prairies, city neighborhoods in Olympia and Lacey, and along wetlands, lakes, and the Deschutes River. The southern 10 miles are exceptionally rural and scenic—and simply divine during the autumn months thanks to an abundance of deciduous trees.

GET MOVING

The Chehalis Western Trail follows a good portion of the old Chehalis Western Railroad line. This was a logging railroad that ran from the 1920s to the 1980s between Weyerhaeuser tree farms near the now-defunct company town of Vail and a log dump on Woodard Bay. From here the logs were rafted to mills in Everett. You can check out a portion of the old log dump by following the nearby Whitham Road Trail in the Woodard Bay Natural Resources Conservation Area (Trail 11).

Below is a brief description of the Chehalis Western Trail from north to south. The trail is marked every half mile. The first half mile of the trail is actually now the Overlook Trail (see Trail 11). The official Chehalis Western Trail starts 0.5 mile from the northern trailhead (privy available). Follow it south through a cedar grove, passing underneath Woodard Bay Road. The way then follows a fairly straight, forested corridor passing rural residences and farms. At milepost 3 (2.5 miles from the northern trailhead), the trail bends left at a wetland, coming to the South Bay Road trailhead at milepost 3.5.

At this and all road crossings, use caution. Now continue primarily through forest-skirting, semirural neighborhoods. After crossing 26th Avenue Northeast, the trail enters Olympia and begins bordering tract housing developments. At milepost 6, cross busy Martin Way East via an overpass. Then right afterward, cross busier I-5 via a bigger overpass. The trail now skirts commercial developments on the Olympia-Lacey city line. At milepost 6.5, cross busy Pacific Avenue Southeast via an overpass—then shortly beyond come to a trail roundabout with the Woodland Trail (see Trail 13), which runs east and west across Lacey and Olympia.

The Chehalis Western Trail continues south, crossing 14th Avenue Southeast and coming to the Chambers Lake

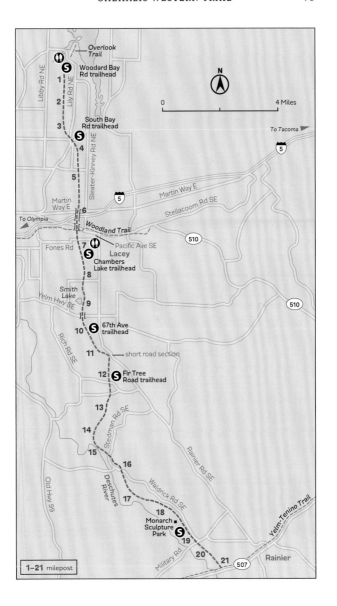

Maples line the trail and add golden hues in autumn.

trailhead—a major trail access point with restrooms and ample parking. The trail passes more residences before coming along a large wetland on the left and Chambers Lake Park on the right. It's a nice greenbelt in an area that is rapidly developing. Take a break at one of the benches overlooking the lake—and look for birds.

The trail then skirts newer housing developments on the left and remnant rural patches on the right. At milepost 9, come to a pretty stretch along Smith Lake (more of a bog). Here a short trail leads among towering conifers to the Rotary overlook—a great spot for a lunch break. Farther south the way cuts through more residential developments before crossing the Yelm Highway on an overpass at milepost 9.5. At milepost 10, reach the 67th Avenue trailhead, another major trail access (but lacking privies).

From this point on, the trail cuts through a more rural setting. At milepost 11, the trail makes an unpaved and potentially muddy left turn to bypass an active rail line. It then goes under the rail line and briefly utilizes the shoulder of busy Rainier Road Southeast before returning to a peaceful paved path. The way now is primarily through mixed conifer and deciduous forests that are absolutely gorgeous come October.

At milepost 12 come to the Fir Tree Road trailhead—a major access point complete with picnic tables and a privy. The trail soon afterward crosses 89th Avenue Southeast and Spurgeon Creek. Traverse attractive forests and wetlands and a rare-on-this-route cut—as most of the terrain has been pretty level. At milepost 15 come along the Deschutes River and one of the prettiest stretches of this trail. A bench overlooking the river invites a break.

Soon afterward cross Stedman Road Southeast, and near milepost 16 cross Waldrick Road Southeast, which has parking but no facilities. The trail then parallels a dirt road and rail line before bending left—then right—and passing beside some small ranches. The way then parallels the rail line again and runs alongside Waldrick Road at a few points. At milepost 18.5, the trail traverses the 80-acre Monarch Sculpture Park (privy available). The sculpture grounds are currently closed to the public, but they will hopefully open again soon if the Creekside Conservancy (a local land conservation and environmental education outreach organization) acquires it.

At milepost 19, the trail once again crosses Waldrick Road. Soon afterward it crosses Military Road. It then traverses open prairie (not choked with invasive Scotch broom) and groves of handsome Garry oaks. The South Puget Sound prairies and oak forests are among the most threatened ecosystems in Washington (see sidebar "Too Many Houses on the Prairie" in Trail 26). Enjoy good views here too of Crawford Mountain to the south. The way then crosses the Willamette Meridian—but you won't see it or know it (see Trail 14)—and traverses the Deschutes Prairie Preserve, a restored natural area owned by the Center for Natural Lands Management.

Just beyond milepost 21, the Chehalis Western Trail merges with the Yelm–Tenino Trail. The original rail line continued farther south—but this is the end of the line for the trail.

Head back to your start—or turn left or right on the paved Yelm–Tenino Trail for more exploring.

GO FARTHER

If you want to get in a long run or can arrange a shuttle for a one-way trip, extend your trip by continuing on a section of the Yelm–Tenino Trail (see Trail 29). Check out the excellent trails in nearby LBA Park, opened as this book was going to press.

13 Woodland Creek Park and Woodland Trail

DISTANCE:	Up to 5.2 miles one-way
ELEVATION GAIN:	Up to 160 feet
HIGH POINT:	200 feet
DIFFICULTY:	Easy
FITNESS:	Walkers, runners
FAMILY-FRIENDLY:	Yes and stroller-friendly, but be cautious at road crossings
DOG-FRIENDLY:	On-leash
AMENITIES:	Interpretive signs, restrooms, benches, play equipment, picnic tables and shelter
CONTACT/MAPS:	City Of Olympia Parks and Recreation and City of Lacey Parks and Recreation; map available online
GPS:	N 47° 02.323", W 122° 47.543"

GETTING THERE

Driving: From Olympia, head north on Interstate 5 to exit 108A in Lacey. Then drive south on Sleater-Kinney Road NE for 0.3 mile. Turn left onto Pacific Avenue SE and proceed for 0.2 mile to a traffic circle. Then continue on Lacey Boulevard SE (a one-way road going east) for 1.1 miles to another traffic circle. Now once again head east on Pacific Avenue SE for 0.6 mile, turning right at a senior center into Woodland Creek Community Park. Continue a short distance to parking and the trailhead.

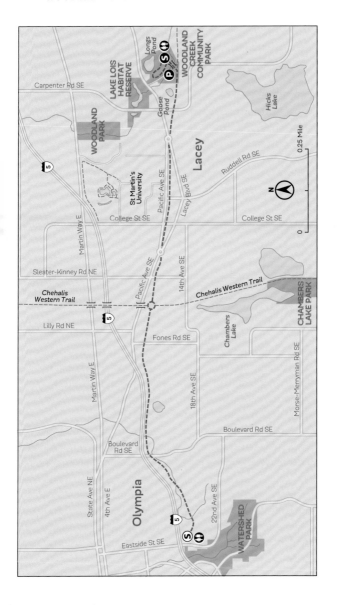

Transit: Woodland Creek Community Park is serviced by Intercity Route 67; the Olympia Woodland Trail west trailhead is serviced by Intercity Route 94.

A paved path connecting Lacey with Olympia, this trail caters primarily to bicycle commuters. Much of the way parallels busy roads and travels through commercial areas—but the trail's eastern and western ends traverse quieter terrain and a couple of peaceful parks. The walking is good at both ends, and the entire trail makes for a great running route off of the streets. The Woodland Trail intersects the Chehalis Western Trail about midway, offering distance runners an add-on for long training runs. And walkers looking for just a short, unhurried workout can get it at Woodland Creek Community Park.

GET MOVING

Lacey's Woodland Creek Community Park is a wonderful place to take the young kids or the pup out for a walk. A couple of short paved paths lead from the park's large parking areas to grassy shores and a fishing dock on placid little Longs Pond. The 72-acre park, along with the adjacent Lake Lois Habitat Reserve, protects important riparian habitat along Woodland Creek. After walking along the pretty pond, take a 0.2-mile paved path, crossing Woodland Creek on a bridge and reaching the paved Woodland Trail.

A rail-trail, the Woodland Trail's current eastern end lies just 0.1 mile to the left. It is possible to continue walking in that direction, following the rail bed, but the going can be tough as this section of trail is currently unimproved. If you do explore, in 0.5 mile you'll reach an old trestle (not advisable to cross) spanning Woodland Creek near Long Lake. There are plans (check with the Woodland Greenway Trail Association) to eventually develop the trail east more than 2.5 miles to State Route 510. But for now, plan on walking or running west on the well-built rail-trail that is currently in place.

Bridge over Woodland Creek

The Woodland Trail continues west all the way to Watershed Park in Olympia. Pass a water retention area and skirt Goose Pond before coming to a crossing of busy Carpenter Road Southeast. Exercise extreme crossing at this and other road crossings along this route—sadly, drivers aren't always attentive. The trail continues through a much more urban corridor of residences and commercial establishments.

At about a half mile from the connector trail at the Woodland Creek Community Park, come to another busy road crossing—this one involving negotiating a roundabout at busy Lacey Boulevard Southeast and Pacific Avenue Southeast. The trail now parallels Pacific Avenue. After another half mile, pass by St. Martin's University, whose attractive campus offers some pleasant walking opportunities (see "Go Farther" below).

The Woodland Trail continues west, coming to a crossing with College Street Southeast 1.5 miles from the park connector trail. Shortly beyond, another roundabout crossing needs to be negotiated before coming to busy Sleater-Kinney Road Northeast. At 2.1 miles from the park connector trail, the Woodland Trail intersects the Chehalis Western Trail (Trail 12) at a trail roundabout. You can roam north or south on this paved rail-trail or keep traveling west on the Woodland Trail—now in Olympia and referred to as the Olympia Woodland Trail.

The path skirts south of a handful of busy plazas before paralleling I-5. Here a connector trail leads left to Fones Road Southeast. The Woodland Trail continues past more residences before traveling through a forested corridor—albeit a noisy corridor due to the adjacent freeway. Exercise caution here, as this is the site of many homeless encampments and some drug use. Park officials have begun to take actions to make this trail safe and clean.

The trail slowly descends, terminating at Eastside Street Southeast 5 miles from the Woodland Creek Community Park connector trail. You can continue walking or running by crossing Eastside Street and following a trail into Olympia's Watershed Park (Trail 2).

GO FARTHER

The St. Martin's University campus offers peaceful walking, especially when classes are not in session. Walk the paths and service roads of the attractive Catholic university to Abbey Way at the northern end of the campus. Here you can wander on peaceful paths through a field and around a few small ponds. There is also a paved path that connects College Street Southeast to Martin Way East. It parallels I-5, so don't expect a quiet walk. Be sure to be respectful of students and residences on the campus and follow all university rules and regulations.

14 William Ives Trail

DISTANCE:	2.6 miles roundtrip
ELEVATION GAIN:	Up to 100 feet
HIGH POINT:	220 feet
DIFFICULTY:	Easy
FITNESS:	Walkers, runners
FAMILY-FRIENDLY:	Yes
DOG-FRIENDLY:	On-leash
AMENITIES:	Restrooms, benches, play equipment
CONTACT/MAPS:	City of Lacey Parks and Recreation; no map online
GPS:	N 47° 05.026", W 122° 45.126"

GETTING THERE

Driving: From Olympia or Lacey, follow Interstate 5 north to exit 111. Turn left onto Marvin Road NE and proceed 0.4 mile north to a roundabout. Exit right onto Willamette Drive NE and continue 1.7 miles to Meridian Neighborhood Park on your right. Park here for the trailhead.

The William Ives Trail travels through a 35-acre pocket greenbelt within the planned developments of Lacey's Meridian Campus community. Used primarily by local residents taking their dog for a walk and area school children out on a short bike ride, the trail is lightly traveled. Amble through a remnant patch of forest harkening back to the not-so-distant past when this entire area was a tree farm.

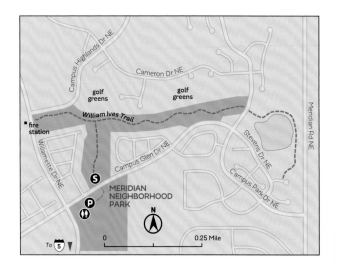

GET MOVING

Find the trailhead for the William Ives Trail just east of the neighborhood park's pavilion. The trail is unmarked and may be confusing to find. The path bends to the north, reaching Campus Glen Drive Northeast in 0.1 mile. Alternatively, you can walk the sidewalk on Campus Glen Drive from the park to this point. From here the trail is obvious. Follow it north through a green wedge between housing developments. It's wide enough that you won't feel like you're in suburbia.

At 0.3 mile come to a junction at a viewpoint looking north to an adjacent golf fairway. The way left climbs a little, ending in 0.1 mile near a fire station on Willamette Drive Northeast. You want to go right on a slightly rolling path through salal and Douglas firs. The trail traverses a narrow greenway slicing through a neighborhood and a fairway. At 0.9 mile come to Campus Park Drive Northeast. Carefully cross the road and continue on the trail, slowly descending to a storm retention pond. The path swings around the pond and heads south, paralleling Meridian Road Northeast. At 1.3 miles the trail ends in a subdivision (no parking). Turn around and retrace your route back to your start.

By this time you may be wondering, just who the heck is William Ives? If you missed the sign along the trail, here's the scoop: William Ives was one of three surveyors who, in 1851, laid out the Willamette Meridian and Base Line near Portland in the Oregon Territory (which included Washington at the time), enabling the establishment of the Donation Land Act and facilitating settlement. Ives was contracted to lay out the meridian all the way from Portland to Puget Sound at the Nisqually Reach. He marked posts every half mile. Meridian Road, just to the east of the trail, follows the original surveyed meridian.

15 Tolmie State Park

DISTANCE:	3 miles of trails
ELEVATION GAIN:	Up to 225 feet
HIGH POINT:	125 feet
DIFFICULTY:	Easy
FITNESS:	Walkers, hikers, runners
FAMILY-FRIENDLY:	Yes
DOG-FRIENDLY:	On-leash
AMENITIES:	Restrooms, benches, interpretive signs, picnic shelter
CONTACT/MAPS:	Washington State Parks; map available online
GPS:	N 47° 07.151", W 122° 46.599"
BEFORE YOU GO:	Discover Pass required; park closed on Monday and Tuesday

GETTING THERE

Driving: From Olympia or Tacoma, take Interstate 5 to exit 111. Then drive north on Marvin Road NE for 3.6 miles. Turn right onto 56th Avenue NE and continue 0.5 mile, bearing left onto Hill Street NE. Proceed 0.4 mile and turn left onto 61st Avenue NE and into Tolmie State Park. Continue 0.4 mile to the second parking area and trailhead.

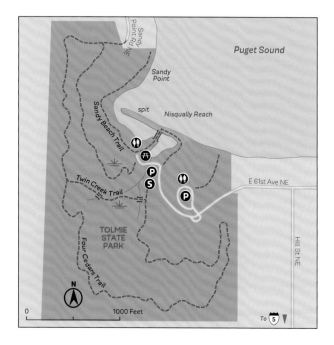

Located on a peninsula on the Nisqually Reach north of Olympia, Tolmie State Park is a popular destination with scuba divers. But hikers, walkers, and runners will find much to their liking too in this peaceful 105-acre park. Despite its compact size, Tolmie harbors 3 miles of trails. Explore a small ravine, coastal bluff, lush cedar groves, and a small creek. Then once you are done with the park's trails, walk a bridge over a lagoon where you can then saunter on a sandy spit.

GET MOVING

This day-use-only state park is popular with locals, but is not on many other Washingtonians' radars. It's worth a trip—and you can easily spend a day here, especially a nice summer one. From the park's second parking area, a handful of trails

BOTANIST, SURGEON, CHIEF FACTOR, POLITICIAN

Born in the Scottish Highlands in 1812, William Fraser Tolmie would go on to live an industrious life as a surgeon, botanist, Hudson's Bay Company (HBC) chief factor, and politician in British Columbia. In 1832, through the recommendation of the famed botanist William Jackson Hooker, Tolmie took a job with the HBC as a medical officer. He arrived at Fort Vancouver in the Oregon Country in the spring of 1833. Soon afterward he traveled north to the Nisqually River Delta to help establish Fort Nisqually (Nisqually House) for the HBC.

In August of 1833, Tolmie—along with two Native guides, Lachalet and Nuckalkat, and three other Native Americans—left for a ten-day "botanizing excursion" to Mount Rainier. Tolmie's main intent was to collect medicinal herbs and observe the mountain's glaciers. Along with his guides, he climbed to the summit of Hessong Rock near the peak that now bears his name. His trip was the first recorded exploration of what is now Mount Rainier National Park. While there, he discovered a new plant species, now called Tolmie's saxifrage.

Tolmie left Fort Nisqually in October of 1833 for other HBC posts throughout western Canada, a trip back to Europe, and a stint back at Fort Vancouver. He returned to Fort Nisqually in 1843 for a sixteen-year stretch, serving for a short period in the Provisional Legislature of Oregon representing the HBC's interest in Puget Sound. And he maintained excellent relations with both the region's Native peoples and the growing influx of American settlers. He supported Chief Leschi in the 1857 trial that led to the chief's wrongful sentencing and execution.

In 1855, he became chief factor at Fort Nisqually but realized that British interests were losing ground in the new Washington Territory. In 1859, he transferred to Fort Victoria on Vancouver Island, where he continued to work for the HBC until 1871. He served in the British Columbia Legislative Assembly and was a strong proponent for Canadian confederation. A lifelong supporter of temperance, Tolmie also advocated for the enfranchisement of women. He studied Native American languages, publishing in 1884 the *Comparative Vocabulary of the Indian Tribes of British Columbia*. He passed away on December 8, 1886.

Twin Creek Trail

depart. Hike, walk, or run them all, creating your own loops, figure eights, or out-and-backs.

Two short trails—one utilizing a bridge over a lagoon—head to a spit offering nice beach walking. Near the picnic shelter, the Sandy Beach Trail takes off north for 0.25 mile along the lagoon, ending at Sandy Point. During low tide you can walk the beach here too. And when the sun is out, enjoy a wonderful view of Mount Rainier. Look out across the reach to Anderson Island and the Key Peninsula.

The Four Cedars Trail takes off from the picnic shelter and makes a grand loop of the park's uplands, returning to the second parking area. It's a great 1.9-mile rolling route that dips into a small ravine and travels over a small bluff and hillside. The vegetation is lush and you'll certainly pass more than four cedars, but there are four (or more) big ones. There are a few big firs too and many big bigleaf maples. Come here in October when the maples add some gold to all of the emerald ferns, lichens, and epiphytes.

The way passes over a few boardwalks in wet depressions along the rolling terrain. The Twin Creeks Trail travels 0.2 mile from the parking lot trailhead to the Four Cedars Trail, offering an option for shorter loops. It's a nice little trail traveling through a lush ravine and crossing over both of the creeks. There are some big cedars along this trail too.

Other trails in the park include a short spur off the Four Cedars Trail to Sandy Point Road Northeast and one from the first parking lot to the shore. And who was Tolmie? Doctor William Fraser Tolmie (see sidebar, "Botanist, Surgeon, Chief Factor, Politician") was a physician, botanist, and fur trader who spent sixteen years with the Hudson's Bay Company at Fort Nisqually, across the reach in what is now Dupont. He is generally regarded as the first non-Native to step foot in what is now Mount Rainier National Park. Yep, Tolmie Peak is named for him too.

16 Billy Frank Jr. Nisqually National Wildlife Refuge

DISTANCE:	3 miles of trails
ELEVATION GAIN:	Minimal
HIGH POINT:	15 feet
DIFFICULTY:	Easy
FITNESS:	Walkers, hikers
FAMILY-FRIENDLY:	Yes
DOG-FRIENDLY:	Dogs prohibited

AMENITIES:	Restrooms, benches, interpretive signs, observation decks, visitor center
CONTACT/MAPS:	United States Fish and Wildlife Service; maps available online and at visitor center
GPS:	N 47° 04.354", W 122° 42.736"
BEFORE YOU GO:	Entrance fee: $3 per four adults; or Interagency Passes accepted
NOTE:	Northern end of the Nisqually Estuary Trail is closed from October to late January for hunting season; all trails closed at dusk.

GETTING THERE

Driving: From Olympia or Tacoma, take Interstate 5 to exit 114. Then turn left from Olympia—or right from Tacoma—and follow Brown Farm Road NE for 0.7 mile to the parking area and trailhead at the refuge visitor center.

Wedged between Olympia and Tacoma, the 3,100-acre Billy Frank Jr. Nisqually National Wildlife Refuge protects one of the last remaining relatively undeveloped river deltas in southern Puget Sound. An important stop for migratory birds, the refuge is home to plenty of species year-round as well. One of the best bird and wildlife viewing spots in the Puget Trough, what really makes visiting Nisqually a sheer delight is its 1-mile elevated boardwalk trail.

GET MOVING

The Billy Frank Jr. Nisqually National Wildlife Refuge was established in 1974 at the mouth of the glacier-fed Nisqually River. Much of the river's delta was part of the Brown Dairy Farm prior to the establishment of the refuge. During this period, more than 5 miles of dikes were built to reclaim salt flats. In 2009, refuge officials removed 4 miles of the dikes, restoring more than 760 acres of tidal salt flats. The large twin barns of the old farm still remain, however, and interpretive signs explain the refuge's history and ecological importance.

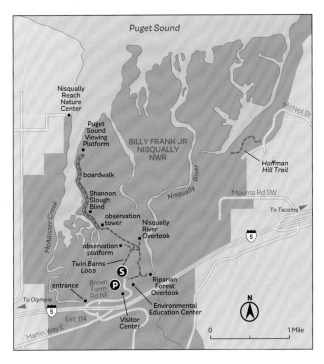

In 2015, the refuge (formerly known as the Nisqually NWR) became known as the Billy Frank Jr. Nisqually NWR. Frank Jr., who died in 2014, was a member of the Nisqually Tribe. Through many acts of civil disobedience, he challenged the state and federal governments to honor the Medicine Creek Treaty (particularly tribal hunting and fishing rights), which was signed in 1854 on land now within the refuge. He was posthumously awarded the Presidential Medal of Freedom by President Obama in 2015. Having the refuge named after him is a fitting honor.

There are basically two trails within the refuge, the Twin Barns Loop and the Nisqually Estuary Trail. You can opt for

Long, snaking boardwalk on the Nisqually Estuary Trail

an easy 1-mile hike on the Twin Barns Loop—or extend your outing with the 1.5-mile Nisqually Estuary Trail. Add the short overlook spurs into the mix and you're looking at a 4.4-mile hike. The entire trail system is wheelchair accessible, but the loop in particular is specifically designed as an ADA trail.

Start your adventure from the Norm Dicks Visitor Center, heading counterclockwise (you can go the opposite direction if you wish) on the Twin Barns Loop. This entire trail is a wide boardwalk skirting sloughs, dikes, and wetland pools that teem with wildlife. In about 0.1 mile, come to a junction with the Riparian Forest Overlook Spur Trail leading 400 feet to a slough along the Nisqually River.

Check out the slough, and then continue on the main loop under giant cottonwoods and maples, coming to another junction at 0.3 mile. First head right a few hundred feet for a good look at the Nisqually River. Then return to the junction and continue hiking the loop—now heading west. At a little over 0.5 mile, come to the historic Twin Barns. Check out the interpretive panels and wildlife viewing areas. More than three hundred species of birds, amphibians, and mammals inhabit the refuge.

Now head onto the Nisqually Estuary Trail, following a dike for the first 0.5 mile, then come to a 1-mile-long snaking elevated boardwalk. It is one of the most unique trails within the state and a pure delight to walk. The boardwalk will take you out into the delta, providing excellent wildlife viewing opportunities and good views of Anderson Island and the Tacoma Narrows. When the tide is out, you'll walk over glistening and gurgling mud and salt flats. It's one of the best times for bird-watching. Depending on the season, look for eagles, dunlins, sandpipers, falcons, merlins, purple martins, and geese. Return often for different sightings.

Follow the boardwalk back to the Twin Barns and complete the loop by walking past more waterfowl- and amphibian-rich wetland pools.

GO FARTHER

In nearby Dupont, you can hike the Hoffman Hill Trail along the eastern boundary of the refuge. It provides some good views of the delta.

Next page: *Flower-lined trail leading up Little Larch Mountain (Trail 21)*

CAPITOL STATE FOREST

Rising to the southwest of Olympia, the heavily forested Black Hills are composed of rolling, gentle peaks. The highest summits are just over 2600 feet. But the relief is prominent due to their close proximity to the Puget Sound Basin and Chehalis River valley. Shrouded in green and stroked with smooth contours, these hills look like they belong in Virginia or Pennsylvania. But they're a unique part of the Washington landscape.

The basaltic Black Hills take their name from a Native American term, *klahle*, describing the dark shadows cast by the ever-changing cloud patterns blown in from the coast. Fires and widespread logging swept through in the early part of the twentieth century. During the Great Depression, the state authorized repurchase of the cutover lands.

Today, the Washington State Department of Natural Resources (DNR) manages more than 90,000 acres of the Black Hills as the Capitol State Forest. Known locally as the Cap Forest, it's a working forest providing a steady stream of timber (converted to income for the state's schools). However, since 1955 the forest has also been managed for recreation. The more than 100 miles of trails traversing Cap Forest are in essence divided in two—the northern half open to motorized recreation, the southern half nonmotorized. Almost all trails are open to hikers, mountain bikers, and equestrians—though there are a few hiker-only trails. (And the motorized trails are actually motor-free [and horse-free] from December 1 to April 30.) Cap Forest also has four campgrounds.

This book includes detailed descriptions of nearly all of the forest's nonmotorized trails. An excellent map can be purchased through DNR and is also sold at area outdoor retailers. Or you can download it to your smartphone using the Avenza PDF Maps Mobile app (visit www.dnr.wa.gov/capitol for instructions).

While this forest may lack the ruggedness of Mount Rainier and Olympic national parks, it offers plenty of surprises—from sweeping views to quiet valleys, plenty of history, and (thanks to scores of volunteer groups) a very well-maintained trail system.

17 | McLane Creek

DISTANCE:	1.5 miles of trails
ELEVATION GAIN:	Up to 25 feet
HIGH POINT:	150 feet
DIFFICULTY:	Easy
FITNESS:	Walkers, hikers
FAMILY-FRIENDLY:	Yes and stroller-friendly; parts ADA-accessible
DOG-FRIENDLY:	On-leash
AMENITIES:	Restrooms, benches, interpretive signs, picnic shelter
CONTACT/MAPS:	Washington DNR, South Puget Sound Region Office; basic map online; Capitol State Forest map available at area outdoor retailers
GPS:	N 47° 00.062", W 123° 00.190"
BEFORE YOU GO:	Discover Pass required

GETTING THERE

Driving: From exit 104 on Interstate 5 in Olympia, head west on US Highway 101 for 1.8 miles, taking the Black Lake Boulevard exit. Take a left at the light, and proceed south on Black Lake Boulevard SW. In 3.5 miles, the road turns west, becoming 62nd Avenue SW. Continue another 0.7 mile to a stop sign. Turn right onto Delphi Road SW and continue for 0.8 mile. Then turn left into the McLane Creek Demonstration

Forest. Proceed for 0.4 mile (passing the Forestry trailhead at 0.3 mile) to the trailhead.

One of the finest nature trails in the Puget Sound region, hikers and walkers of all ages—and especially children—will love the easy and wildlife-rich trails of McLane Creek. Via wide, well-groomed paths and sturdy boardwalks, explore the grassy shores of a beaver pond, gurgling McLane Creek, and quiet woodlands. Look for a myriad of birds and explore an old logging railroad grade.

GET MOVING
Washington DNR needs to be commended on this hiker-only trail system. It was clearly developed with environmental sensitivities and meant to make it easier for people to connect with nature. This is a great place to green-bond youngsters and older folks discovering the natural world for the first time.

The McLane Creek Nature Trail consists of a 1.1-mile outer loop, a 0.3-mile connector trail (allowing for a shorter 0.6-mile loop), and a couple of spur trails to lakeshore and

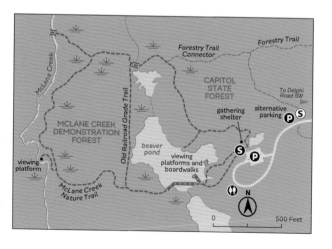

Viewing platform on the beaver pond

creek overlooks. The trail system is short and easy, yet so delightful it's not unusual to see folks making multiple loops. And with interpretive plaques and observation decks along the way, McLane Creek is meant to be savored. Time of day and season will dictate which critters you might observe on this trail. Keep your senses keen and you should see plenty anytime you visit. And while running isn't prohibited here—it's better to run elsewhere so wandering toddlers and preoccupied birdwatchers can enjoy a more peaceful and less hurried environment.

Going clockwise, the main loop trail starts off by skirting a large beaver pond. In springtime the wetland is transformed into a musical marsh thanks to a chorus of blackbirds and an ensemble of tree frogs performing regularly. Cattails and pond lilies punctuate the nutrient-rich wetland. Soon you'll encounter a shortcut. Once part of the Mud Bay Logging Company's rail line, this trail offers more good views of the beaver pond—and perhaps a peek of the beavers themselves.

The main trail darts into a dark and gloomy forest of cedar, hemlock, giant maples, monster stumps, and over-your-head devil's club. Follow it, heading to McLane Creek—the trail once crossed over it twice, but seasonal flooding had the final say. A nice observation deck now stands where the first crossing once stood—and farther along, a spur (the old trail) leads to the second (now only) bridge crossing, where in fall you can look for spawning salmon. The old hemlock tunnel—a favorite of many a child—unfortunately met its demise in a winter storm, but the surrounding mossy woods still conjure up a mystical aura that is sure to keep the youngins enchanted.

The main loop then traverses a skunk cabbage patch before returning to the beaver pond. Here you can go right on the Old Railroad Grade Trail or head left to continue on the main loop. Cross the pond's outlet and continue wandering along the willow-, alder-, and cascara-lined wetland. Pass a trail heading left to the Forestry Trail (see "Go Farther" below) and a trail heading right to an observation point on the pond. Then cross a small creek while rounding a marshy cove and return to your start.

GO FARTHER

Check out the nearby Forestry Trail. While it's not nearly as interesting as the McLane Creek trails, this 1-mile loop is often deserted, assuring you peaceful forest ambling. You can access it from a trailhead 0.1 mile east of the McLane Creek trailhead or take a 0.2-mile connector trail from the main McLane Creek loop. The Forestry Trail crosses a small creek, passes through a small cut, and travels primarily through second-growth forest.

18 Mima Falls

DISTANCE:	6-mile loop
ELEVATION GAIN:	400 feet
HIGH POINT:	575 feet
DIFFICULTY:	Moderate
FITNESS:	Hikers, runners
FAMILY-FRIENDLY:	Yes, but beware of mountain bikers and equestrians
DOG-FRIENDLY:	On-leash
AMENITIES:	Privy, picnic tables
CONTACT/MAPS:	Washington DNR, South Puget Sound Region Office; basic map online; Capitol State Forest map available at area outdoor retailers
GPS:	N 46° 54.210", W 123° 03.830"
BEFORE YOU GO:	Discover Pass required

GETTING THERE

Driving: From Olympia, head south on Interstate 5 to exit 95. Then drive west on Maytown Road SW for 2.9 miles to a major intersection in Littlerock. Continue west on 128th Avenue SW for 0.8 mile. Then turn left onto Mima Road SW. Proceed for 1.3 miles and turn right onto Bordeaux Road SW. Continue 0.7 mile and turn right onto Marksman Street SW. After 0.8 mile, bear left to the Mima Falls trailhead entrance and continue 0.3 mile to the trailhead.

A popular destination within the Capitol State Forest, Mima Falls makes for a good rainy-season hike, when visitation is low and the creek level is high. The falls are small and lack a wow-factor, but there are some big trees and a wildlife-rich wetlands along the way. By doing the suggested loop, you'll get a good workout in too, with some decent mileage and a little elevation gain. Otherwise, it is a pretty easy out-and-back to the falls.

GET MOVING

The trailhead (elev. 250 feet) used to start from a camp-ground—but it was decommissioned a few years back, which explains the odd set-up with its loops and separate parking areas. Camping is now verboten here—but picnicking is fine, so claim a spot with a table for an après-hike feast. However, it might be a little loud here (especially on the weekends) with the sound of gunshots, as the Evergreen Sportsmen's Club is just outside the forest boundary.

Start your hike or run on the Mima Falls East Trail, a wide and well-trodden path through a fairly recent cut. Like the other trails in the Capitol State Forest, this trail is well maintained by volunteer groups, and it is well signed. While this trail's

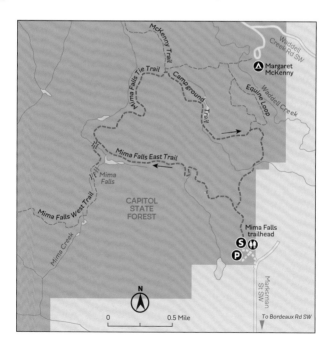

Mima Falls

start in a cut is fairly unappealing, it gets better—so carry on. At 0.4 mile, come to a junction with the Campground Trail. If you're doing the loop, you'll be returning on this trail.

Keep left on the Mima Falls East Trail and soon cross DNR road E-9000. Continue across more cutover land and at about 0.8 mile welcome a forest canopy. Now skirt a wetland, dip a little to cross a creek, and climb a little. Then cross another cut—and soon afterward welcome a mature forest with some big firs and cedars. The way now continues on a fairly level course, brushing alongside a big wetland.

At 1.9 miles, reach a junction with the Mima Falls Tie Trail. This is your return route if you're doing the loop. But first, the falls—which lie just a short ways ahead. So carry on left, soon coming to a big bridge spanning a tributary of Mima Creek. Walk a little farther and at 2.2 miles reach another bridge (elev. 375 feet) over the tributary. Here, just before the bridge, locate a primitive trail taking off near a picnic table. Use extreme caution on this short but rough and steep path leading to an excellent view of the small, pretty waterfall fanning over a ledge. In summer, it's not much, but in winter, it's quite showy indeed.

Now head back to the junction with the Mima Falls Tie Trail. Here, at 2.5 miles, you have the choice to return directly back to your start for a roundtrip hike of 4.4 miles—or head left on the Mima Falls Tie Trail for a loop, adding 1.6 miles and some ups and downs.

Through a uniform forest of mature second-growth, the Mima Falls Tie Trail steadily climbs, cresting a 575-foot ridge. It then gives up about 75 feet and quickly regains it. The trail then heads downward once again, reaching a junction (elev. 375 feet) with the Campground Trail at 3.7 miles. The way left leads a short distance to McKenny Trail, popular with equestrians. From there, it's 1.4 miles right to the Margaret McKenny Campground—or 5.5 miles left to the Fall Creek trailhead (see Trail 20).

You want to go right on the Campground Trail, passing the terminus of the E-9000 road and following alongside a creek in a small ravine. On a generally downhill course, skirt wetlands and pass through an old cut. Pass an old trail sign too, placed here before the trail system was upgraded and renamed a few years ago. Cross the E-9000 road twice and come to a junction at 5 miles with the Equine Loop. Don't even think about hiking this trail, as it is equestrian-only.

You want to continue right through tall timber. Pass another wetland and emerge in scrappy forest. Ignore an unmarked trail leading left to private property. The way climbs a little before slightly descending and reaching a familiar junction at 5.6 miles. Now back on the Mima Falls East Trail, it's 0.4 mile left back to your start.

GO FARTHER

From Mima Falls, you can continue hiking on the Mima Falls West Trail. The way follows the tributary a short distance before turning west and heading over a small ridge. It then drops to cross Mima Creek before climbing once again. The way crosses the D-4000 road and enters the Lost Valley Creek drainage, coming to the Lost Valley Trail (see Trail 20) 4.7 miles from the falls.

19 Bob Bammert Grove

DISTANCE:	1.1 miles roundtrip
ELEVATION GAIN:	325 feet
HIGH POINT:	600 feet
DIFFICULTY:	Moderate
FITNESS:	Hikers
FAMILY-FRIENDLY:	Yes
DOG-FRIENDLY:	On-leash
AMENITIES:	Benches
CONTACT/MAPS:	Washington DNR, South Puget Sound Region Office; basic map online; Capitol State Forest map available at area outdoor retailers
GPS:	N 46° 53.758", W 123° 05.791"
BEFORE YOU GO:	Discover Pass required

GETTING THERE

Driving: From Olympia, head south on Interstate 5 to exit 95. Then drive west on Maytown Road SW for 2.9 miles to a major intersection in Littlerock. Continue west on 128th Avenue SW for 0.8 mile. Then turn left onto Mima Road SW and drive 1.3

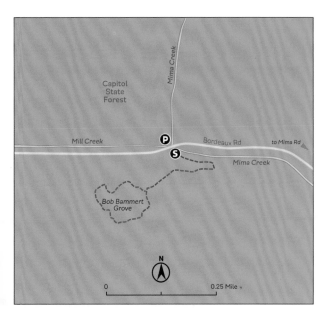

miles. Next turn right onto Bordeaux Road SW and continue 2.5 miles (1 mile past Capitol State Forest Bordeaux Entrance) to the trailhead (elev. 275 feet) on your left. Park on your right.

In this sprawling state forest, where stands have been cut-over two or three times, big, old trees are a rarity. But tucked on a steep slope above Mima Creek is a surviving patch of towering timber. Hike a quiet trail up a lush hillside to the Bob Bammert Grove. Then dawdle on a loop through old-growth cedars, hemlocks, and Douglas firs. It's a window into the not-so-faraway past when the entire surrounding Black Hills were shrouded in big trees like these.

GET MOVING

Not only does this trail deliver some old-growth trees—it's hiker-only too. So no concerns about dodging mountain

Rare old-growth forest in the Capitol State Forest

bikers or yielding to horses on this one. Take your time, let your mind drift, and let your senses absorb the peaceful surroundings. The way immediately starts climbing, traversing a steep herbaceous slope above Mima Creek.

Admire the babbling creek below as you step over a series of smaller feeder creeks. Beneath a thick emerald canopy keep climbing, soon reaching a switchback. Then climb some more, coming to a bench and a junction at 0.3 mile. Here a loop trail takes off through the Bob Bammert Grove. The grove was named for a longtime DNR forest manager—it was Bammert who was responsible for keeping it off the chopping block.

Go either way—but I prefer counterclockwise because of a short, steep section that is easier to ascend than descend.

Take your time on the loop, admiring a few old-growth Douglas firs and some big, old western red cedars as well. You'll cross a creek a couple of times too, which adds a nice ambience to the grove. So does the lush understory of ferns, mossy shrubs, and vine maples. The maples add touches of gold to the verdant surroundings come October. After you close the loop, return the way you came—which is much easier in this direction.

20   Lost Valley Loop

DISTANCE:	8-mile loop
ELEVATION GAIN:	800 feet
HIGH POINT:	1125 feet
DIFFICULTY:	Moderate
FITNESS:	Hikers, runners
FAMILY-FRIENDLY:	Yes, but note trail is open to horses and bikes
DOG-FRIENDLY:	On-leash
AMENITIES:	Restrooms, picnic tables
CONTACT/MAPS:	Washington DNR, South Puget Sound Region Office; basic map online; Capitol State Forest map available at area outdoor retailers
GPS:	N 46° 56.245", W 123° 07.890"
BEFORE YOU GO:	Discover Pass required

GETTING THERE

Driving: From exit 104 on Interstate 5 in Olympia, head north on US Highway 101 for 1.8 miles, taking the Black Lake Boulevard exit. Turn left at the light, and proceed south on Black Lake Boulevard SW. In 3.5 miles the road turns west, becoming 62nd Avenue SW. Continue another 0.7 mile to a stop sign. Turn left here on Delphi Road SW and proceed for 2.1 miles, bearing right onto Waddell Creek Road SW.

Continue, entering the Capitol State Forest, and bear right onto Sherman Valley Road SW in 2.7 miles. Now follow

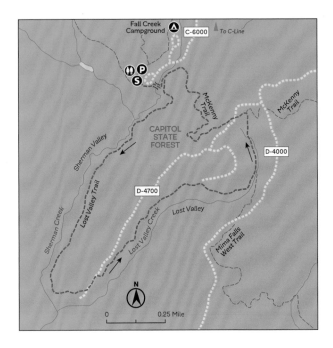

this road, which becomes the C-Line in 1.4 miles. Stay on the C-Line (pavement ends in 0.1 mile) for 2.5 miles (road becomes paved again at 2.2 miles), turning left onto C-6000. Then follow this bumpy-at-times road 1.8 miles to its end (just past a campground) at the Fall Creek trailhead (elev. 550 feet).

A mid-distance loop popular with area mountain bikers, the Lost Valley Loop is ideal for a good trail run or day hike. The way travels through mature forest in the Sherman Creek valley—then up the Lost Valley through mixed-age stands. It then crests a small ridge and descends, traversing clear-cuts granting good views of Capitol Peak, before wrapping it up with a little creekside wandering.

GET MOVING

This loop used to be one of the most delightful hiking experiences in the Cap Forest. But several years ago, much of the trail in the Lost Valley was rerouted away from Lost Valley Creek. This meant no more traveling through lush river bottom forest and meadows—and no more putzing along trestle remains from one of the forest's old logging railroads. It was one of my favorite sections of trail in the forest—and sadly, it is gone. Flooding and logging have claimed the old trail—so don't even think about trying to find it. The newer trail? Less appealing—but it's built well and still fun to run or hike.

Start your hike or run by following the McKenny Trail south through big timber, soon coming to a bridged crossing of Sherman Creek. Skedaddle over the creek and come to a junction at 0.2 mile with the Lost Valley Trail. You'll be returning on the McKenny Trail on your left—so continue right. The trail is well signed, well maintained, and a delight to run or hike. On a rolling course, the way hugs hillsides above the creek. Cross a lot of tumbling side creeks. In spring, the way is lined with flowering corydalis. In autumn, clusters of vine maples create golden archways.

Pass mile and half-mile posts from when this trail was known as the Mima Porter Trail. Hike through future and past harvest areas. At about two miles, you'll reach a 520-foot low point. The way then bends left to climb along a ridge, leaving the Sherman Valley behind. At 3 miles come to a logging road. Turn left and follow the road a short distance, returning to the trail (elev. 920 feet) at 3.4 miles.

The way now winds through uniform forest, dropping about a hundred feet and crossing a creek before climbing again. Lost Valley and its beautiful creek are lost below—this new route goes nowhere near the waterway. The trail follows old road segments, traversing scrappy forest and a recently harvested area. It then goes up and down a couple of times through thick vegetation, coming

Stately trees along the Lost Valley Trail in the Sherman Creek Valley

to a junction (elev. 970 feet) with the Mima Falls West Trail at 5.3 miles.

Head left, climbing along the Lost Valley Creek (finally in view)—then cross it and enter a clear-cut. At 5.7 miles, reach a junction (elev. 1120 feet) with the McKenny Trail. The way right travels 4.7 miles to the Margaret McKenny Campground. You want to go left—soon reentering woods—and shortly afterward cross the D-4700 road. Now in mature second-growth forest, begin a long descent into the Sherman Creek valley. The way makes a long switchback (perfect for bikes and horses), crossing a creek and passing some tall trees. It then enters a recent clear-cut granting an excellent view of Capitol Peak. At 7.8 miles, reach a familiar junction with the Lost Valley Trail. Turn right and return to your start in 0.2 mile.

GO FARTHER

Make this loop much longer by following the Mima Falls West Trail east from the Lost Valley Trail junction. After 5 miles, follow the Mima Falls Tie Trail 1.2 miles to the Campground Trail (see Trail 18). Turn left and in 0.1 mile reach the McKenny Trail. Then turn left again and follow this trail 5.4 miles to the Lost Valley Trail junction near Sherman Creek. This 17.2-mile loop makes for a satisfying long hike or trail run.

21 Little Larch Mountain

DISTANCE:	4 miles roundtrip
ELEVATION GAIN:	750 feet
HIGH POINT:	1340 feet
DIFFICULTY:	Moderate
FITNESS:	Hikers, runners
FAMILY-FRIENDLY:	No; trail is heavily used by mountain bikes
DOG-FRIENDLY:	On-leash
AMENITIES:	Benches
CONTACT/MAPS:	Washington DNR, South Puget Sound Region Office; basic map online; Capitol State Forest map available at area outdoor retailers
GPS:	N 46° 56.365", W 123° 07.578'
BEFORE YOU GO:	Discover Pass required

GETTING THERE

Driving: From exit 104 on Interstate 5 in Olympia, head north on US Highway 101 for 1.8 miles, taking the Black Lake Boulevard exit. Turn left at the light, and proceed south on Black Lake Boulevard SW. In 3.5 miles the road turns west, becoming 62nd Avenue SW. Continue another 0.7 mile to a stop sign. Turn left here on Delphi Road SW and proceed for 2.1 miles, bearing right onto Waddell Creek Road SW. Continue, entering the Capitol State Forest, and bear right onto Sherman Valley Road SW in 2.7 miles.

Now follow this road, which becomes the C-Line in 1.4 miles. Stay on the C-Line (pavement ends in 0.1 mile) for 2.5 miles (road becomes paved again at 2.2 miles), turning left onto C-6000. Then follow this bumpy-at-times road 1.6 miles to an unmarked trailhead (elev. 590 feet) on your left, just before a bridge over Fall Creek.

This fun little trail sees a fair amount of mountain bike use—but very little foot traffic. With its flow and deep banks, it is definitely a bike trail. But come on a weekday, and you may have it to yourself. Enjoy a large, open flat that bursts with flowers in the spring, a mature forest, and a decent view of the Waddell Creek valley. Just don't expect any larches—little or big.

GET MOVING

From the unassuming trailhead, start gently climbing. The trail travels through a young forest of firs and vine maples on a bench above Sherman Creek. Ignore a side path leading left to the road. At 0.4 mile enter an old cut and pass by an interesting platform in a lopped tree. Is it used by mountain bikers filming their comrades?

Now enjoy easy wandering across a flat cutover area where feisty new greenery is returning life to the former forest floor. In springtime, an array of showy flowers—both native and nonnative (such as foxgloves, which are toxic but pretty nonetheless)—brighten up the landscape as well. At 0.9 mile come to a junction (elev. 750 feet). Here a spur leads left 0.1 mile to an alternative trailhead on C-6000. This trailhead—located 0.7 mile north of your start—is used mostly by bikers wishing to avoid the flatter lower section of this trail.

Continue right and soon cross C-6200. Then reenter forest and begin steadily climbing. The trail is flowy—a mountain biker's delight. Traverse tall timber and come to the first of several trail splits that have up- and downhill sections for bikers. Stick to the uphill sections. The way grows steeper with

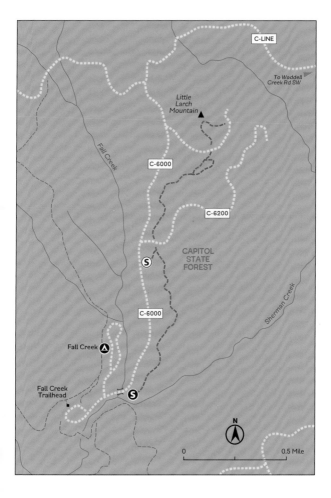

tight switchbacks. At 1.4 miles, reach an unmarked junction. The way left is a steep and short route that meets back up with the longer and gentler route heading right. Take the path right and meet back up with the shorter route at 1.6 miles. Veer right and continue upward as the trail becomes steeper.

Cross a logging road, and soon afterward crest the broad, 1340-foot summit of low-lying Little Larch Mountain. At 2 miles reach an overlook complete with a bench and railing. Here look out over a clear-cut to a decent view of the Waddell Creek valley, Mount Rainier, and the Cascades. The trail continues another 0.2 mile, dropping 100 feet and reaching a logging road. It holds little interest for hikers—but follow it out and back if you care to add some distance. Otherwise, enjoy the view and return the way you came.

And if you're wondering about those larch trees—they don't exist. Western larches grow on the eastern slopes of the Cascades and throughout the forested regions of Eastern Washington. Alpine larches grow at high elevations in the North Cascades, also east of the crest. But early lumbermen in the Northwest referred to noble firs as Oregon larches. Why? Fir had low timber value back then. In Washington, noble firs grow primarily at mid-elevations in the southern Cascades and can also be found at higher elevations in southwest Washington's Willapa Hills. But the Black Hills? No noble firs. So no faux larches either, making this peak and its larger counterpart—2660-foot Larch Mountain, the highest peak in the Black Hills—doubly misnamed peaks!

22 Capitol Peak

DISTANCE:	17-mile loop
ELEVATION GAIN:	2300 feet
HIGH POINT:	2659 feet
DIFFICULTY:	Difficult
FITNESS:	Hikers, runners
FAMILY-FRIENDLY:	No; trail shared by bikes and horses
DOG-FRIENDLY:	On-leash
AMENITIES:	Privy, picnic tables

CONTACT/MAPS:	Washington DNR, South Puget Sound Region Office; basic map online; Capitol State Forest map available at area outdoor retailers
GPS:	N 46° 56.267", W 123° 07.884"
BEFORE YOU GO:	Discover Pass required

GETTING THERE

Driving: From exit 104 on Interstate 5 in Olympia, head north on US Highway 101 for 1.8 miles, taking the Black Lake Boulevard exit. Turn left at the light, and proceed south on Black Lake Boulevard SW. In 3.5 miles the road turns west, becoming 62nd Avenue SW. Continue another 0.7 mile to a stop sign. Turn left on Delphi Road SW and proceed for 2.1 miles, bearing right onto Waddell Creek Road SW.

Continue, entering the Capitol State Forest, and bear right onto Sherman Valley Road SW in 2.7 miles. Now follow this road, which becomes the C-Line in 1.4 miles. Stay on the C-Line (pavement ends in 0.1 mile) for 2.5 miles (road becomes paved again at 2.2 miles), turning left onto C-6000. Then follow this bumpy-at-times road 1.8 miles to its end (just past a campground) at the Fall Creek trailhead (elev. 550 feet).

Capitol Peak is the second-highest (just misses highest by one foot) summit in the Black Hills. Its summit is marred with towers, but its views are grand—from Rainier to the Pacific and a whole lot more. This Cap Forest classic offers a long day hike or challenging trail run involving a big loop from Fall Creek to Cap Peak. The distance is long, but the grade is generally gentle. And the payoff, aside from a lot of burned calories? Views, attractive forest, cascading creeks—and even more views!

GET MOVING

This loop is bisected by roads at numerous points, making much shorter options possible if 17 miles is too daunting.

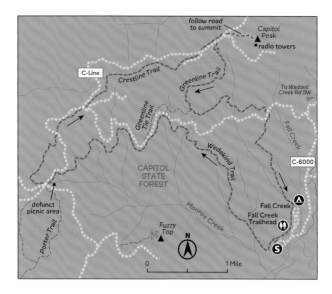

Otherwise, accept the challenge, and show those mountain bikers that anyone can do this loop on two wheels—two feet, however, that's an accomplishment!

From the trailhead, head north on the Greenline Trail, coming to a junction at 0.2 mile. Here a trail leads right to the Fall Creek Campground. The Greenline—your return route—continues straight. You want to go left on the Wedekind Trail. Now begin a long, gentle ascent, passing through a patchwork of mature standing timber, younger regenerating stands, and harvested areas. At about 1.3 miles cross road C-5300.

Continue meandering on well-built and maintained tread, making many bridged creek crossings—including an exceptionally attractive one in a pretty ravine. At about 4 miles, traverse a cut providing sweeping views south of Mounts Adams and St. Helens and the Goat Rocks. After crossing a new skid road, reenter forest, coming to a junction (elev. 1500 feet) with the Greenline Tie Trail at 4.3 miles. Here it is possible to hike or run right 1.4 miles to the Greenline Trail—then return to the trailhead for a 9.3-mile loop.

The grand Cap Peak loop continues left. Come to a big bridge spanning a small creek. Then, after passing through a new cut, the way follows one of the many old logging railroad beds crisscrossing the forest. At about 6 miles, reach a bridge spanning a creek at a slick rock cascade. At 6.5 miles, reach a trail junction and the C-Line and D-1000 roads at the defunct Wedekind Picnic Area (elev. 1875 feet). Here the Porter Trail (Trail 25) heads south. You want to cross the C-Line and follow the Crestline Trail north. At 6.8 miles, bear right where the abandoned old Greenline Trail heads left.

Now enjoy easy ridgeline cruising through silver firs and a lush green carpet. The way dips once on its generally gentle ascent. At 7.7 miles, cross the C-Line (elev. 2000 feet). Alternating between fir forests lined with oxalis (pretty white blooms in late spring) and raspberry-cloaked "balds" reminiscent of the southern Appalachians, the trail is a pure delight to travel. Teaser views of the Cascades, Olympics, and Willapa Hills are had along the way.

At 8.2 miles, cross the C-Line again—here at its junction with C-4000 left, and C-4010 right. The trail resumes a few hundred feet up C-4010 on the left. Now climb some more, bearing right at a junction with an abandoned trail. Continue through more fir forest and shrubby openings on a gently rolling ridgeline. Cross another road. The trail, now paralleling two roads, climbs a small knoll—then descends to where the roads intersect. Here at 10.1 miles, cross the road left and follow the trail through huckleberries paralleling the C-4000.

At 10.5 miles reach a junction with the Greenline Trail (elev. 2300 feet). But before returning on that trail, walk the road straight a short distance to a three-way junction. Take the gated middle road and climb steeply 0.6 mile to the 2659-foot summit of Capitol Peak, the second-highest summit in the

Clear-cuts on Cap Peak provide expansive views.

Black Hills. The highest summit, 2600-foot Larch Mountain, can be seen to the north. It's trail-less and treed—but not with larches—and lacks views.

Here on Cap Peak, beneath a skyline of communications towers, look out to soak in sweeping views. To the east are the Cascades, from Mount Baker to Mount Adams. Rainier is directly in front of you, rising above the Bald Hills. Extending to the north are the finger peninsulas and inlets of the South Sound. To the west, the Satsop Towers rise above the Chehalis Valley, while the Olympics and Pacific Ocean can be seen in the distance.

Now retrace your steps back to the Greenline Trail junction. With 11.7 miles now under your hiking belt, you have a shorter, albeit steeper, return to your start. Following tight switchbacks, the way loses elevation rapidly. It then makes a long traverse, crossing new logging roads and coming to a clear-cut with expansive views east. Another round of tight switchbacks awaits you before coming to a junction with the Greenline Tie Trail (elev. 1600 feet) at 13.6 miles.

Continue left, soon passing an interesting biker route option. Cross a spur road, follow another old logging rail line, and pass over another cascading creek before crossing the paved C-Line at 15 miles. Continue descending, soon coming to a skid road. The trail follows this road left for a short distance—then enters a clear-cut. The trail comes to another road—head right on it, soon return___ ___ trail. The way then crosses a creek and pass___ _____ ___leading to the Fall Creek Campground___ ___ ___ ___ ___ to a familiar junction with the ___ ___ ___ ___ ___raight ahead and return to your ___ ___ ___ ___ ___hat sports drink and chocolate ___ ___ ___ ___ ___le!

23 Fuz___

DISTANCE:	1.4 miles roundtrip
ELEVATION GAIN:	400 feet
HIGH POINT:	1760 feet
DIFFICULTY:	Easy
FITNESS:	Hikers
FAMILY-FRIENDLY:	Yes
DOG-FRIENDLY:	On-leash
AMENITIES:	Benches
CONTACT/MAPS:	Washington DNR, South Puget Sound Region Office; basic map available; Capitol State Forest map available at area outdoor retailers
GPS:	N 46° 56.245", W 123° 10.512"
BEFORE YOU GO:	Discover Pass required

GETTING THERE

Driving: From exit 104 on Interstate 5 in Olympia, head north on US Highway 101 for 1.8 miles, taking the Black Lake Boulevard exit. Take left at the light, and proceed south on

A rare patch of old-growth forest in the Capitol State Forest

Black Lake Boulevard SW. In 3.5 miles the road turns west, becoming 62nd Avenue SW. Continue another 0.7 mile to a stop sign. Turn left on Delphi Road SW and proceed for 2.1 miles, bearing right onto Waddell Creek Road SW.

Continue, entering the Capitol State Forest, and bear right onto Sherman Valley Road SW in 2.7 miles. Now follow this road, which becomes the graveled C-Line in 1.5 miles. Then follow this good (mostly gravel, sometimes paved) road for 7 miles to a major junction (just beyond a borrow pit). Bear left, continuing on the C-Line for 1.6 miles to a junction at the old Wedekind Picnic Area site. Turn left onto the D-1000 and drive

1.1 miles, bearing left onto the D-1500. Then continue 0.5 mile to the trailhead (elev. 1650 feet) on your left.

This is a short and sweet hike with a few little treats. Its long approach and general remoteness make it a good candidate for solitude. It's hiker-only too—so no bombing mountain bikers. There are some good views of Capitol Peak and a good portion of the Cap Forest too. But this trail's real joy? A remnant patch of old-growth forest within this sea of harvested woodlots.

GET MOVING

Compared to other trails within the Capitol State Forest, the path to Fuzzy Top will seem primitive. The tread is narrow—and ferns and salal encroach upon it in spots. But this lightly traveled trail is generally in good shape, requiring perhaps just a few kicks to get some branches off the tread.

Start by climbing about 50 feet up a forested knoll. Then descend 150 feet to a saddle at the edge of a recent cut.

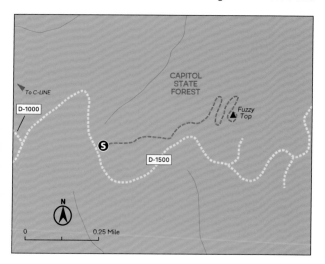

Briefly hike across the cut as you begin to climb again. Enjoy views out to Capitol Peak. Soon enter forest—then genuine old-growth. How it survived in this working forest is a miracle. Pass giant hemlocks, cedars, and Douglas firs. From a distance, the big trees perched on this little knoll above clearcuts and young forest give the appearance of a fuzzy top.

Eventually reach the 1760-foot summit of Fuzzy Top, where a little loop swings through the ancient grove of trees. There are a couple of neglected benches along the loop. Brush the needles aside—then sit and savor the serenity of this special little forest.

24 Porter Falls

DISTANCE:	1.6 miles roundtrip
ELEVATION GAIN:	200 feet
HIGH POINT:	380 feet
DIFFICULTY:	Easy
FITNESS:	Hikers
FAMILY-FRIENDLY:	Yes
DOG-FRIENDLY:	On-leash
AMENITIES:	Privy at nearby campground
CONTACT/MAPS:	Washington DNR, South Puget Sound Region Office; basic map online; Capitol State Forest map available at area outdoor retailers
GPS:	N 46° 58.685", W 123° 15.388"
BEFORE YOU GO:	Discover Pass required

GETTING THERE

Driving: For the easiest access from Olympia (avoiding long approaches on dirt roads), use the following directions: Follow US Highway 101 north to State Route 8, and take this west to US Highway 12. (It's possible to reach US 12 from SR 8 via the Mox Chehalis Road, saving some distance.) Then drive 6 miles east on US 12 to the hamlet of Porter. Turn left at the

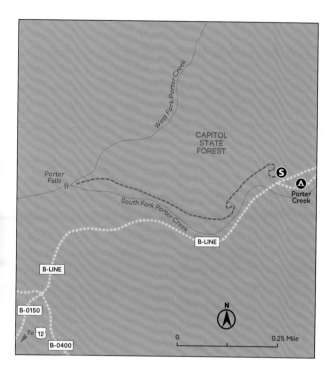

Porter Saloon (where I imagine you can get a porter) onto Main Street. Proceed two blocks and turn left onto Porter Creek Road.

Then follow this paved road for 2.9 miles to where it becomes the graveled B-0150 road. Continue north (ignore road on right) for 0.5 mile to a junction with the B-Line and B-0400. This is the western trailhead for the Porter Trail (trail is on the north side of B-0400; see Trail 25). For the Porter Falls trailhead you want to continue north on the B-Line for 0.9 mile (just past Porter Creek Campground entrance) to the trailhead (elev. 290 feet) on your left. Parking is tight. More parking is available near campground entrances.

Cascades above Porter Falls

Follow this quiet, hiker-only trail through stately moss-covered trees to a small, hidden basaltic chasm. Here at the confluence of the South and West Forks of Porter Creek, one branch cuts through a cleft while the other plunges over a ledge into a big punchbowl. It's a pretty scene year-round—but especially during the rains of winter, when the little falls lets out a little roar.

GET MOVING

Starting by an old water pump, follow the trail into a dark forest and begin climbing. The way ascends about a hundred feet via a couple of switchbacks. It then traverses a steep slope before descending again steeply, giving up that hundred feet of elevation gain. The trail then comes upon South Fork Porter Creek. Here the old approach heads left. You want to keep right, hiking through a tunnel of big maples along the tumbling creek.

The trail then comes up along the tumbling West Fork Porter Creek. Continue hiking, coming to the confluence of the two branches and Porter Falls at 0.8 mile. It's a pretty little spot that warrants some exploration—but use caution, especially with children, as the ledges can be slippery. Shaded by luxuriant greenery, the West Fork plunges into a basaltic punchbowl basin, while the South Fork careens through a tight basaltic chasm. Check out the potholes in the ledges. There's a small upper falls above Porter Falls too. In winter this little cascade can rage. By late summer it can soothe a weary soul.

25   Porter Trail

DISTANCE:	13 miles one-way
ELEVATION GAIN:	400 feet
HIGH POINT:	2050 feet
DIFFICULTY:	Moderate
FITNESS:	Hikers, runners
FAMILY-FRIENDLY:	Yes
DOG-FRIENDLY:	On-leash
AMENITIES:	None
CONTACT/MAPS:	Washington DNR, South Puget Sound Region Office; basic map online; Capitol State Forest map available at area outdoor retailers
GPS:	N 46° 56.903", W 123° 11.668"
BEFORE YOU GO:	Discover Pass required

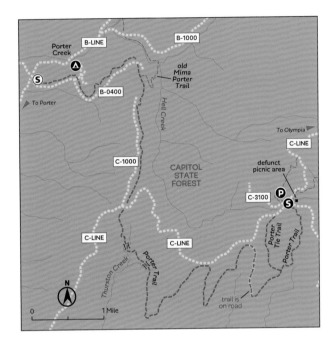

GETTING THERE

Driving: From exit 104 on Interstate 5 in Olympia, head west on US Highway 101 for 1.8 miles, taking the Black Lake Boulevard exit. Turn left at the light, and proceed south on Black Lake Boulevard SW. In 3.5 miles the road turns west, becoming 62nd Avenue SW. Continue another 0.7 mile to a stop sign. Turn left on Delphi Road SW and proceed for 2.1 miles, bearing right onto Waddell Creek Road SW.

Continue, entering the Capitol State Forest, and bear right onto Sherman Valley Road SW in 2.7 miles. Now follow this road, which becomes the graveled C-Line in 1.4 miles. Then follow this good (mostly gravel, sometimes paved) road for 7 miles to a major junction (just beyond a borrow pit). Bear left, continuing on the C-Line for 1.6 miles to the trailhead (elev. 1850 feet) at a junction by the defunct Wedekind Picnic Area site. Parking available on the west side of the C-Line.

The Porter Trail is the quietest of Capitol State Forest's long-distance, nonmotorized trails. Start along the Cap Forest crest and traverse ridges and valleys in the forest's western reaches, descending to the Porter Creek valley. The trail is in excellent shape and includes a couple of surprises. There's a Sitka spruce grove, a sweeping view of the Chehalis River valley, a wildlife-rich wetland, and a couple of old logging railroad grades. Best of all—you'll probably have the entire trail all to yourself!

GET MOVING

This trail is best done as a one-way route, east to west, due to its distance and elevation change (this direction also takes advantage of an elevation drop of more than 1700 feet). Once, it was possible to do a loop by utilizing the old Greenline Trail—but logging and floods have obliterated sections of that no-longer-maintained trail. You'll need to leave a car (or arrange for a shuttle) at the trail's western end, near the Porter Creek Campground (see Trail 24 for directions). Of course, you can always do this trail as an out-and-back for any distance, from either direction. And if you are an ultra-runner, go for the whole distance out and back—completing nearly a marathon round-trip.

On the trail, you're more likely to run into equestrians than mountain bikers (it's open to both)—if you run into anyone at all. Of course, expect to encounter a few wild four-legged critters.

The trail starts by climbing through a Sitka spruce grove (more common on the coast) along a ridge to a 2050-foot high point. Then the way begins its long descent—briefly following an old logging railroad grade. At 1.3 miles, come to a junction (elev. 2000 feet) with the Porter Tie Trail. This trail

Hikers admire a mature stand of second-growth forest.

heads right 0.9 mile back to the C-Line. From there, you can walk right on the road a short distance back to the trailhead, for a loop of around 2.5 miles.

You want to go left, traversing a ridge above the North Creek valley. At 2.3 miles the trail emerges on a logging road. Follow this road through a large recent cut offering excellent views over the Chehalis River valley and to the Doty Hills. The road trail makes a big, wide swing around a drainage—coming to the C-2700 road and returning to trail again at 3.4 miles. The trail then climbs a little before resuming its long, gentle descent. It makes a wide swing around a ridge, traversing clear-cuts and crossing skid roads in the process. It then follows an old railroad line before crossing Thurston Creek at around 5 miles.

Continue across more cuts and cross the C-2000 road at 5.9 miles. Then travel through more Sitka spruces before crossing more cuts and logging roads. The way then climbs a little—and then heads downward once more, coming to a sprawling wetland. Next make two bridged crossings of Thurston Creek tributaries before climbing 200 feet through an attractive mature forest punctuated with some big mossy stumps.

At 7.7 miles, cross the C-Line (elev. 1150 feet). Walk a short distance up the C-1000 in front of you and look for the trail right. Pass more big trees—and stumps that used to be even bigger trees. The trail marches north along the rim of a ravine housing Hell Creek. Wonder if it ever gets cold enough here for Hell to freeze over?

At 10.3 miles reach an unmarked junction (elev. 1100 feet). The way right is the old Mima Porter Trail, leading steeply down to the valley below and to a horse camp. It used to access the old Greenline Trail (since abandoned), allowing for a big loop. DNR officials hope to someday build a new trail to reinstate a loop option here. Until then go left and begin a rapid descent. Pass a horse bypass trail providing a gentler grade. In wet weather take care not to slip on the clay tread, which gets really slick.

Enjoy some good views of surrounding hills and ridges and the Porter Creek valley below as you wind down toward it. Cross the B-0400 road and then parallel it. Cross logging roads three more times and emerge in a clear-cut. At 13 miles, reach the Porter Trail's western trailhead (elev. 335 feet) at the junction of the B-Line, B-0150, and B-0400 roads. Get into your shuttle car and go retrieve the car you left at the start. And sleep well after completing your long hike or run.

Next page: *Old barn at Scatter Creek Wildlife Area*

SOUTH THURSTON COUNTY

Offering a distinct contrast to the urbanized northern reaches of the county, Thurston County's southern flanks are rural, consisting of tree farms and family farms. Here, away from the bustling cities along Puget Sound, find small-resource-dependent communities, historic hamlets, lakeside developments, and encroaching suburbia. The county's southeast section consists of the Bald Hills and Cascade Mountains foothills—but has virtually no trails.

Instead look to the broad valleys bisected by the Black, Chehalis, and Deschutes rivers. In the prairies and oak groves wedged between the Black Hills and Bald Hills, find public lands offering good hiking, running, and walking opportunities. Several long-distance rail-trails cut through the countryside, offering good wanderings. One of the area's most interesting places is Deschutes Falls. The county acquired this naturally significant property in the early 1990s, and recently opened it to the public. While there's little as far as trails go in the 154-acre park, the falls thundering in a tight gorge is a beautiful sight to behold.

26 Mima Mounds Natural Area Preserve

DISTANCE:	2.8 miles roundtrip
ELEVATION GAIN:	25 feet
HIGH POINT:	240 feet
DIFFICULTY:	Easy
FITNESS:	Walkers, hikers
FAMILY-FRIENDLY:	Yes and partially ADA-accessible
DOG-FRIENDLY:	Dogs prohibited
AMENITIES:	Privy, picnic tables, interpretive displays
CONTACT/MAPS:	Washington DNR, South Puget Sound Region Office; basic map online; Capitol State Forest map available at area outdoor retailers
GPS:	N 46° 54.307", W 123° 02.879"
BEFORE YOU GO:	Discover Pass required

GETTING THERE

Driving: From Olympia, head south on Interstate 5 to exit 95. Then drive west on Maytown Road SW for 2.9 miles to a major intersection in Littlerock. Continue west on 128th Avenue SW for 0.8 mile. Then turn right onto Waddell Creek Road SW and proceed for 0.8 mile. At a sign announcing "Mima Mounds Natural Area," turn left. Reach the trailhead in 0.4 mile.

Hike through a landscape that almost appears lunar (except for the vegetation, of course). Weave in and out and even over a few of the hundreds of four-to-six-foot mounds scattered across this prairie and oak savannah environment. How did these mysterious mounds come about? You'll most certainly be pondering this while hiking through this geologically intriguing landscape. Visit in spring when the preserve explodes with purple thanks to a proliferation of camas blossoms. There are plenty of other blossoms too throughout the warmer months.

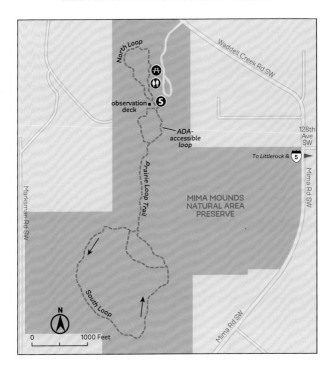

GET MOVING

Most visitors to this National Natural Landmark just visit the observation deck and maybe walk the 0.5-mile paved nature loop. To really appreciate the beauty and mystery of Mima Mounds, take to the longer trail that loops around the 637-acre preserve. By all means, head for the observation deck first to get a look at this bizarre arrangement of "earthen hay bales." Scientists continue to debate the mounds' origins. Was it a period of thaw and freeze preceding the last ice age, causing the land to buckle—or perhaps the work of pocket gophers who have since moved on to haunt golf courses?

Now walk the paved, ADA-accessible path, heading right on this loop and coming to a junction in 0.3 mile with the

A patch of camas in bloom at Mima Mounds

much longer Prairie Loop Trail. Now on a soft-surface path, head into the heart of the mounds. The surrounding forest has encroached on the prairie—invasive plants flourish too, like the dreaded Scotch broom. DNR and volunteers are trying to restore the prairie to the way it appeared when Native peoples periodically set fires to keep vegetation in check.

Nearly all of the South Sound Mima Mounds outside of this preserve have been altered in some way, whether from development and agriculture or by invading nonnative plants. This reserve protects a rare prairie and a host of species dependent on this ecosystem for their survival. Among them are several rare and endangered butterflies, including the Mardon skipper, Puget blue, Taylor's checkerspot, and zerene fritillary.

At 0.6 mile pass an old fence line, a remnant of early farming on the mounds. At 0.7 mile come to a junction. Turn right to follow the South Loop. Soon pass another junction, a shorter loop option. Continue right, hiking the periphery of

TOO MANY HOUSES ON THE PRAIRIE

One of the rarest ecosystems in the Northwest, South Puget Sound prairies are a valuable part of our natural heritage and face a series of threats. Formed by retreating glaciers that left behind gravelly soils favoring grasslands and oak savannahs, these areas were kept open for centuries by Native Americans using controlled burns. The area's first Euro-American settlers were attracted to these lands for homesteading and farming. As settlement increased, agriculture and urbanization converted many of our native prairies into farms, housing developments, warehouses, and shopping centers. Today only 3 percent of the original 150,000 acres of South Sound prairies remain pristine.

Most of the prairies and savannahs that have remained in an undeveloped state are threatened with nonnative invasive species. These plants—in particular the insidious Scotch broom—have replaced native plant species and displaced or eliminated the native fauna dependent on them. Several conservation groups have been active in the South Sound, protecting and restoring these important, vanishing ecosystems.

Among some of the fauna that call the prairies home are Mazama pocket gophers, western gray squirrels, streaked horned larks, western meadowlarks, western bluebirds, Oregon vesper sparrows, sharp-tailed snakes, western fence lizards, western pond turtles, Oregon spotted frogs, and several species of rare butterflies. Among the flora associated with South Sound prairies are groves of Garry (Oregon white) oaks, bunchgrass, camas, golden paintbrush, white-topped aster, rose checkermallow, small-flowered trillium, and Torrey's peavine.

The Center for Natural Lands Management, working with The Nature Conservancy, has been a leader in South Sound prairie conservation and restoration. Visit www.southsoundprairies.org for more information on our threatened prairies. You can visit excellent prairie habitat at the Mima Mounds Natural Area Preserve (Trail 26) and the Scatter Creek Wildlife Area (Trail 27). Thurston County Parks' Black River–Mima Prairie Glacial Heritage Preserve, one of the largest and finest remaining prairies, can only be visited once a year during Prairie Appreciation Day in May. It's worth marking your calendar so you won't miss the opportunity to visit this special preserve.

the preserve. Enjoy views of Mounts Rainier and St. Helens towering in the distance. In 2.1 miles close the loop. Retrace your steps back to the paved loop and head right 0.2 mile, returning to the observation deck. If you're content, return to the parking area. If not—extend your visit by hiking the lightly traveled 0.5-mile North Loop.

The Mima Mounds are exceptionally beautiful in April and May, when prairie flowers such as blue violets, buttercups, shooting stars, and camas paint them in dazzling colors. In summer, the mounds are streaked with various shades thanks to death camas, cinquefoils, woolly sunflowers, harebells, lupines, and others.

27 Scatter Creek Wildlife Area

DISTANCE:	3.2 miles of trails
ELEVATION GAIN:	20 feet
HIGH POINT:	180 feet
DIFFICULTY:	Easy
FITNESS:	Walkers, hikers
FAMILY-FRIENDLY:	Yes, when it is not hunting season
DOG-FRIENDLY:	On leash
AMENITIES:	Privy, interpretive panels, historic buildings
CONTACT/MAPS:	Washington Department of Fish and Wildlife (WDFW), Coastal Region 6; basic map online
GPS:	N 46° 49.664", W 123° 00.445"
BEFORE YOU GO:	Discover Pass or WDFW Vehicle Access Pass required
NOTE:	Active hunting area, wear orange or avoid during hunting seasons; Inner Loop is open to all uses to July 31; Outer Loop, August 1 to March 31

GETTING THERE

Driving: From Olympia, head south on Interstate 5 to exit 88 at Grand Mound. Then head west on US Highway 12 for 0.3 mile and turn right onto Elderberry Street SW. Now follow this road north for 0.2 mile and turn right onto 193rd Avenue SW.

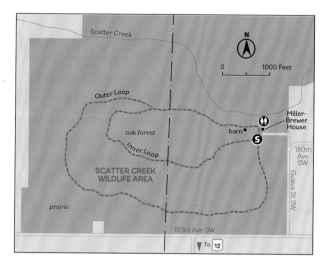

Stay on this road as it bears left onto Guava Street SW, and proceed for 1 mile to an intersection with 183rd Avenue SW. Turn right, and then immediately turn left, following Guava Street SW north for 0.4 mile to Scatter Creek Wildlife Area. Drive to the west end of the large lot for the trailhead, near the site of the historic Miller-Brewer House.

When it's not hunting season, this Washington Department of Fish and Wildlife (WDFW) property is quiet, seeing just a few locals out walking their dogs. Walk a long or short loop (depending on when you visit) through a gorgeous prairie and oak savannah along the lazy Scatter Creek. Wildlife and flowers are abundant in season, including elk and camas. And on sunny days the views when clouds are gone are sweeping, from the Black Hills to Mount Rainier.

GET MOVING
One of three units totaling 926 acres managed as the Scatter Creek Wildlife Area by the WDFW, this parcel includes

The historic Miller-Brewer House graced this wildlife area until 2017.

hiker-only trails and a couple of historic structures. Located on a glacial outwash plain formed by ice age glaciers a mile and a half thick—this parcel is now shrouded in prairie and oak groves. It's part of a mosaic of protected lands within the Black and Chehalis River valleys, containing some of the last remaining native grasslands and oak forests in Western Washington (see sidebar, "Too Many Houses on the Prairie" in Trail 26). WDFW's management here includes restoring the prairie to a presettlement state by using prescribed burns, removing invasive plants, and replanting native species.

This parcel is particularly diverse in that it also contains riparian forest and wetland communities along a mile of Scatter Creek. The trails are practically level and as easy as it gets when it comes to terrain. But you'll want to walk slowly, taking your time and observing and possibly identifying a mosaic of birds, butterflies, and blossoms. Be sure to watch for ticks too—they usually bloom right when the first flowers are budding.

Near the trailhead, the historic Miller-Brewer House once stood in a grove of stately Garry (Oregon white) oaks. This Greek Revival house was built in 1860, one of the longest-standing, box-frame style homes in Washington from the territorial period. And it remained at its original location until it was destroyed in a wildfire in 2017. In the 1850s, George and Marita Miller arrived by wagon from Oregon to take a Donation Land Claim. Miller and his family farmed this prairie parcel. George also became a territorial representative and county commissioner.

In 1873, the Millers sold this house to Reece Brewer, who had crossed the Oregon Trail as a teenager. Brewer farmed this tract with his family and also served as a county commissioner and territorial representative. Reece's son Fred arranged to have the home and land sold to the Washington State Game Department (now the WDFW) in 1963, one year before his passing.

Take a hike around this culturally and naturally significant property. Walk a wide old farm road west. On your left is a big red barn. On your right is oak-lined Scatter Creek. Pass this way in early spring, and blossoming camas add touches of purple to the surrounding greenery. The area's vegetation is reminiscent of the Willamette Valley in Oregon. Pass by some mounds and a powerline. Enter a large field and come to a junction. Whether you go right on the long outer loop or left on the shorter, inner loop will depend on the time of year.

The outer loop continues as a double track, traveling through fields along the periphery of the property. The inner loop walks along the periphery of a forested tract within the middle of the open plain. On this loop, marvel at beautiful oaks—and, in season, a wide array of prairie flowers (including arrowleaf balsamroot, rare in Western Washington). Both loops return to the trailhead.

GO FARTHER

You can also hike a mile-plus loop trail on the northern tract of the wildlife area, accessible from Case Road Southwest (reached by heading east on 183rd Avenue Southwest).

28 Millersylvania State Park

DISTANCE:	More than 8 miles of trails
ELEVATION GAIN:	Up to 200 feet
HIGH POINT:	290 feet
DIFFICULTY:	Easy
FITNESS:	Walkers, hikers, runners
FAMILY-FRIENDLY:	Yes
DOG-FRIENDLY:	On-leash
AMENITIES:	Restrooms, interpretive panels, historic buildings, picnic tables, camping area
CONTACT/MAPS:	Washington State Parks; map available online
GPS:	N 46° 54.581", W 122° 54.414"
BEFORE YOU GO:	Discover Pass required

GETTING THERE

Driving: From Olympia, head south on Interstate 5 to exit 99. Then turn left and follow State Route 121 for 4.2 miles. Turn right (west) into the state park entrance, and immediately come to a trailhead with a parking area on your left. More day-use parking is available at picnic areas.

Hike, run, or walk through 842 acres of towering old-growth forest and rich productive wetlands just minutes from the state capitol. Dubbed Millersylvania (meaning "Miller's wooded glade") by early land owner John Miller, this large tract was bequeathed to the state in 1921. In 1935, the Civilian Conservation Corps (CCC) developed it into a lovely state park. There's camping, swimming,

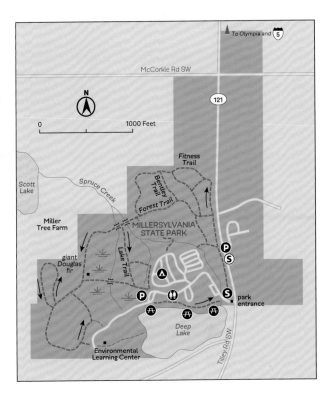

boating, and picnicking—and more than 8 miles of trail to explore here.

GET MOVING

Despite having a large interconnecting trail system, the park's campground and waterfront on Deep Lake appear to be the bigger draws. There are always locals out walking their dogs and running the park's trails—but these paths never get crowded. There are a lot of loop options available and a little hill work too, if you want it. The online map not very useful—but the ones posted throughout the park are decent, with some ballpark mileages on them too. Trails are well marked and signed.

If you've never been here before and need a good introduction to the park's trails—or you're looking for a good varied run or hike around the park—consider the following 4.2-mile loop. Locate the trailhead across the road and head north through a corridor of towering firs skirting a wetland. At 0.4 mile, come to an old orchard and parking area (alternative start). Continue north, now on the Fitness Trail (stop at the heart rate–raising stations if you care to), crossing a service road and reaching the northern boundary of the park.

The trail bends left. Stay right at three upcoming intersections (the Fitness Trail loop and Bentley Trail). Eventually, the near-level trail will bend south. Continue through a grove of big, ancient trees, reaching a junction with a service road called the Forest Trail at 1.4 miles. Now turn right onto this old road-turned-trail and continue hiking or running under a canopy of mature timber. Pass a trail leading left 0.4 mile to the campground. Then cross a bridge over Spruce Creek and pass the Lake Trail (which can be muddy), leading 0.4 mile left to Deep Lake.

Stay straight and soon come to another bridge—this one spanning a wetland. The way now starts to climb. At 1.9 miles bear left. The way right leaves the state park, entering the Miller Tree Farm. Do check out the kiosk set up there. The Millers are excellent stewards of their land and were the Washington State Tree Farmers of the Year in 2013.

Continuing in a stand of magnificent ancient trees, reach a junction at 2.1 miles near a colossal Douglas fir. Despite having its top broken off, it's probably one of the largest trees in the park. You'll be returning to your start via the trail left—but first continue right for two short loops. Immediately pass a trail on your left (you'll be returning on it) and come to a four-way junction at 2.2 miles, near an old water tower set among big maples.

Boardwalk across wetlands near Deep Lake

Go right, first dropping 50 feet and then regaining them on a short loop, returning you to the water tower at 2.6 miles. Then head down the other trail, dropping about 75 feet and coming to a spur to the park's environmental learning center at 3 miles. Then traverse a wet meadow and climb back up, reaching a familiar junction at 3.2 miles. Head right, and then immediately head right again at the colossal Doug fir.

Now descend the wooded hillside and come to the start of a long and interesting boardwalk cutting across a large wetlands expanse. Stay right at a junction where the Lake Trail travels left through a grove of cedars. Soon cross over Spruce Creek and reach the boat launch parking area at 3.8 miles. Now walk paths along Deep Lake, traveling through picnic areas and groves of giant, ancient trees. Pass beautiful structures (now in need of restoration) built by the CCC during the Great Depression. At 4.2 miles return to your start.

29 Yelm–Tenino Trail

DISTANCE:	Up to 14 miles one way
ELEVATION GAIN:	Up to 200 feet
HIGH POINT:	430 feet
DIFFICULTY:	Easy
FITNESS:	Walkers, runners
FAMILY-FRIENDLY:	Yes and stroller-friendly, but be aware of bicycles
DOG-FRIENDLY:	On-leash
AMENITIES:	Interpretive signs, restrooms, benches, picnic tables
CONTACT/MAPS:	Thurston County Parks; map available online
GPS:	N 46° 56.519", W 122° 36.501"

GETTING THERE

Driving: There are several trailheads and access points along this trail. Major trailheads with parking can be found at the following locations.

Yelm trailhead: From Olympia, follow Interstate 5 north to exit 111. Then drive State Route 510 for 13 miles to Yelm, turning right (just before a stoplight at the junction with State Route 507) onto Railroad Street SW. Proceed one block to the trailhead and parking.

Rainier trailhead: From Lacey, head south on College Street SE for 3.4 miles to a junction with Yelm Highway. Then continue straight, now on Rainier Road SE. After 10.2 miles, Rainier Road SE becomes Minnesota Street North. Continue for 0.2 mile and turn left onto Rochester Street West. Drive

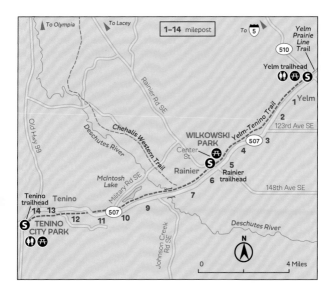

one block to trailhead parking at Wilkowski Park, on your right.

Tenino trailhead: From Olympia and Tumwater, follow I-5 south to exit 102. Then head left on Trosper Road SW for 0.1 mile. Next turn right onto Capitol Boulevard SE, which becomes Old Highway 99, and drive 11 miles to a junction with SR 507 in Tenino. Turn right onto SR 507 and drive 0.4 mile. Then turn left onto S. Olympia Street and reach the trailhead and parking at Tenino City Park in two blocks.

Transit: The Yelm trailhead is serviced by Intercity Route 94 from Olympia and Lacey.

Walk or run part or all of this delightful, 14-mile paved rail-trail across southern Thurston County. The way once hosted part of the Prairie Line Railroad, which connected Kalama to Tacoma and operated for more than a century. Now you can chug through oak forests, prairies, farmlands, and along an undeveloped lakeshore. Pass through small communities and the site of a once-thriving mill town. Span the Deschutes River and enjoy some good views of big ole Mount Rainier hovering in the east too.

GET MOVING

Although this trail parallels SR 507, the highway remains out of view for most of the way. Sample this trail from either end or at its midsection, near the small community of Rainier. The Yelm end is definitely the busier section, with dog walkers, runners, and families on bicycles. But this trail never gets crowded—except during the annual Seattle to Portland (STP) bicycling event in June, when it's closed to the public to allow thousands of tights-clad cyclists to pass through.

Below is a brief description of the Yelm–Tenino Trail from east to west. The trail is marked every half mile, starting with milepost 0 at the Yelm trailhead. Pass a restroom, picnic shelter, and a skateboard park popular with local teens. Then travel through a pocket park before crossing Mosman Avenue. Pass a subdivision and enter the countryside.

The path travels through a corridor of cottonwoods, maples, and aspens. In autumn it screams yellow. The trail crosses a couple of quiet side roads (but always exercise caution while crossing) and a large sheep farm. At milepost 3.5, the trail veers away from the highway and cuts through a wetland lined with towering cottonwoods. The way then passes through a stand of mature Garry oaks.

After passing beneath a rail line, the trail enters the little city of Rainier and cuts through Wilkowski Park's long, open lawn. Pass a picnic shelter, benches, and some metal sculptures. Cross Center Street and arrive at the Rainier trailhead (with parking) at milepost 5.5. Here you can walk over to nearby establishments for a cold or hot drink, snack, or meal.

The trail then crosses Minnesota Street and continues down a long, open lawn. Pass a spur leading left to schools

Walking the Yelm-Tenino Trail in Rainier

and ballfields. Then traverse woodlots and prairie succumb-
ing to ugly invasive Scotch broom. The way then enters forest
and passes over a grown-over rail bed—part of the original
Chehalis Western logging railroad that went all the way to the
now defunct company town of Vail.

At milepost 7, come to a trail junction. Here the Chehalis
Western Trail bears right on its 20.5-mile journey to Woodard
Bay (Trail 12). Continue straight through a corridor of uniform
young conifers—growing since the rail line was abandoned in

Trail along McIntosh Lake

the late 1980s. Just after milepost 7.5, cross the Deschutes River on a wooden bridge. Pause to admire it before carrying on to the most scenic stretch of trail.

At milepost 9, begin more than a mile of walking or running along the undeveloped south shoreline of McIntosh Lake. Be sure to stop to read the interpretive panel near the Military Road Southeast crossing that describes the mill town that once stood here. Nothing but a few bricks and pilings remain of this community that once housed hundreds of immigrants from Japan and Scandinavia.

After crossing Military Road Southeast, the trail once again runs along SR 507. Here pastoral farmland sprawls south of the highway. Near milepost 11.5, the trail crosses SR 507. Use extreme caution crossing this road, where vehicles often pass at high speeds. The way then traverses forest and wetlands, crossing a couple of creeks along the way.

At milepost 12.5, the trail enters the Tenino city limits and skirts a couple of new housing developments. On the south side of the trail, admire a large wooded tract—the Mill Pond Property, a protected preserve of the Creekside Conservancy. The Conservancy has been active in protecting threatened properties within the Chehalis River Basin. A hiking trail starting at the nearby Tenino City Park traverses this property.

At 13.5 miles, reach the Tenino trailhead (restrooms available) at the city's attractive municipal park. You can continue about 0.5 mile to the trail's end near a historic depot. The park occupies the site of an old sandstone quarry, which has been converted into a swimming area. Definitely check it out—and check out the nearby small city too, with its historic sandstone structures.

GO FARTHER

Combine a long walk or run on this trail with the adjoining Chehalis Western Trail. Or from the Yelm trailhead, cross Yelm Avenue (SR 507) to follow the Yelm Prairie Line Trail. This paved trail is a continuation of the old rail line now utilized by the Yelm–Tenino Trail. The Yelm Prairie Line Trail passes some light industrial areas and a park (with parking accessed via 1st Street) with good views of Mount Rainier. It then crosses 1st Street, passing open terrain. The way then crosses Canal Road Southeast and skirts a housing development before ending at 1.5 miles, just short of the historic Centralia Canal. County officials and trail advocates would like to someday extend this trail by 3.3 miles to Roy in Pierce County. For now, you'll have to call it a walk or run here.

Next page: *Rocky Beach on Oakland Bay (Trail 33)*

SHELTON

Located on Oakland Bay, Shelton is the westernmost city on Puget Sound. A city built on timber (and still supporting a large forestry economy), Shelton also boasts a strong (and succulent) oyster industry. This city of 10,000 has seen hard times with the demise of the timber industry in the 1990s, but its proximity to Olympia, the Olympic Peninsula, and miles of Puget Sound shoreline has attracted a steady stream of new residents.

Shelton's downtown consists of many historic buildings and relics from the days when timber was king in Washington. City center streets offer good walking, and there are a couple of short trails connecting neighborhoods. Shelton lacks large public parks and has only a few short trails. But that is slowly changing. In 2013, the city released a trails plan that, if implemented, will greatly increase trails throughout the city. In the meantime, definitely give the Huff N Puff Trail a go. And there are a few excellent tracts of public lands on the outskirts of the city with trails deserving of your running shoes or hiking boots.

30   **Huff N Puff Trail**

DISTANCE:	1.85 miles of trails
ELEVATION GAIN:	20 feet
HIGH POINT:	230 feet
DIFFICULTY:	Easy
FITNESS:	Walkers, runners
FAMILY-FRIENDLY:	Yes
DOG-FRIENDLY:	On-leash
AMENITIES:	Privy
CONTACT/MAPS:	Mason County government; map available online (Parks & Trails homepage)
GPS:	N 47° 14.229", W 123° 07.182"

GETTING THERE

Driving: From Olympia, head north on US Highway 101 to the Wallace Kneeland Boulevard exit in Shelton. Turn right and

My son and I hit the trail on a rainy morning.

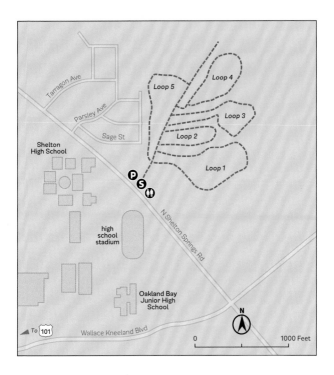

drive east on Wallace Kneeland Boulevard 0.6 mile. Then turn left onto N. Shelton Springs Road and continue 0.3 mile to parking and the trailhead on your right (across from Shelton High School).

Transit: Mason Transit Authority (MTA) Routes 2 and 7

Don't be misled. Huff N Puff sounds like something steep and daunting—not this trail. Here, in a small park across the road from the city's high school, find a wide and wood-chipped, soft-surface, near-level trail snaking through an attractive forest. It's a great trail for a leisurely walk—or a tempo run, perhaps leading to a little huffing and puffing.

GET MOVING

The Huff N Puff Trail is more like a spaghetti heap of small trails. Here five loops intertwine with an old service road. Study the map on the large sign for the layout. Then begin your workout on Loop 1, progressing through the other four. When you've finished, you will have tallied 1.85 miles. Need more of a workout? Do them again in reverse.

While you are running or walking on this path, it may feel like a maze through the mature second-growth. All of this trail distance is packed into just 5 acres of park. If you are out running with a group of friends, you'll be able to catch glimpses of each other through the thin vegetative walls as you double back on the loops.

The trail is practically level, but there are a couple of little dips to add a whoop-de-doo to your run. The forest is quite attractive, consisting primarily of mature cedars and Doug firs. Along Loop 5, a handful of scrubby Garry oaks grow. There's a disc course in the park, so be aware of flying objects. After your run or walk, check out the memorial at the trailhead listing the names of local high school students who died before graduation. It's a sobering tribute.

31 Goldsborough Creek

DISTANCE:	1 mile roundtrip
ELEVATION GAIN:	25 feet
HIGH POINT:	100 feet
DIFFICULTY:	Easy
FITNESS:	Walkers
FAMILY-FRIENDLY:	Yes
DOG-FRIENDLY:	On-leash
AMENITIES:	None
CONTACT/MAPS:	Mason County government; map available online (Parks & Trails homepage)
GPS:	N 47° 12.458", W 123° 07.982"

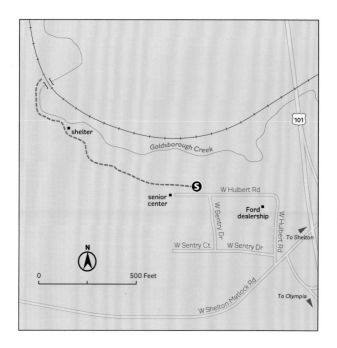

GETTING THERE

Driving: From Olympia, head north on US Highway 101 to the Railroad Avenue exit in Shelton. Turn left on W. Railroad Avenue, which becomes W. Shelton Matlock Road. Pass under the freeway and immediately turn right onto W. Hulbert Road. Continue 0.2 mile and turn left at the Ford dealership. Still on W. Hulbert Road, proceed 0.2 mile to the unmarked trailhead on your right.

Transit: Mason Transit Authority (MTA) Route 9

Walk along a recently undammed creek that's once again spawning salmon. This short trail takes you to several good viewpoints along a series of manmade rapids where salmon can often be seen. But if your fish findings come up short,

Artificial rapids along Goldsborough Creek

there are always birds to watch—particularly kingfishers and mergansers.

GET MOVING

An important creek for Shelton's development, Goldsborough was dammed back in 1885. From millpond to hydro source to water source for a downtown mill, salmon runs were sacrificed for progress. But by the turn of this century, the dam was no longer needed and the current owners, the Simpson Timber Company, arranged for its removal.

The thirty-foot dam came down in 2001, and it didn't take long afterward for salmon, particularly coho, to return. The creek at this point, however, hasn't been completely restored to a natural state. There are now thirty-six low concrete barriers creating a set of rapids. This doesn't impede salmon migration, but it does slow the creek from flooding downstream. Even though these rapids aren't natural, they are kind of cool and add a little water music to your hike. They also make it easier to spot migrating fish.

Start up the wide trail past a gate and pass through an open area before reaching forest. Now follow a single track (which can get muddy during wet periods) toward the creek. While the creek has been enhanced, this trail can use some improvements. Some signage, a replacement for the interpretive sign that has seen better days, and a facelift for the small shelter at the beginning of the rapids would be a good start.

But don't let the condition of the trail discourage you from enjoying this tiny slice of nature just outside of Shelton. In 0.3 mile, come to the creek and its artificial rapids. Take some time to just stop and watch. Then walk upstream, coming to the trail's end at a railroad line. Now turn around and, heading downstream, languidly return to your start.

GO FARTHER

City officials hope to someday build a new stretch of trail along Goldsborough Creek all the way to downtown. Check with the parks department for any new development on this project.

One of the best trails in the area for watching salmon is the Kennedy Creek Salmon Trail. Located near Oyster Bay south of Shelton, this path is owned by the Taylor United Shellfish Company and was developed by the South Puget Sound Salmon Enhancement Group with many partners including Evergreen State College, the Squaxin Island Tribe, and the US Navy Seabees. The trail is only open during November weekends (10:00 AM–4:00 PM), as well as on Veterans Day and the Friday after Thanksgiving. School groups and organizations can make reservations for weekday visits during November. It is a half mile in length and most of it is ADA-accessible. Dogs are prohibited. Visit http://spsseg.org for more information on this wonderful interpretive trail and for directions on how to get there.

32 Lake Isabella State Park

DISTANCE:	More than 4 miles of trails
ELEVATION GAIN:	Up to 100 feet
HIGH POINT:	200 feet
DIFFICULTY:	Easy
FITNESS:	Walkers, hikers, runners
FAMILY-FRIENDLY:	Yes
DOG-FRIENDLY:	On-leash
AMENITIES:	Privy, benches
CONTACT/MAPS:	Mason County government; map available online (Parks & Trails homepage)
GPS:	N 47° 10.117", W 123° 06.610"
BEFORE YOU GO:	Discover Pass required

GETTING THERE

Driving: From Olympia, head north on US Highway 101 to the Olympic Highway (State Route 3) exit in Shelton. Then turn left and travel under the freeway, following W. Golden Pheasant Road for 0.9 mile and turning right onto W. Delight Park Road. Continue for 0.6 mile to the trailhead and parking on your right.

An undeveloped and little-known state park property, Lake Isabella contains several miles of quiet trails and old woods and farm roads to wander. This former farm on the eastern

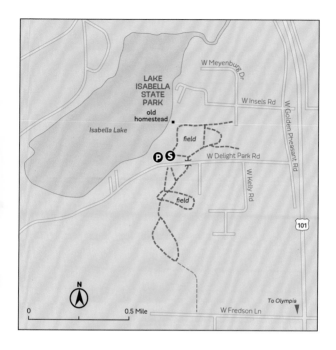

shore of Lake Isabella is now a 182-acre preserve of old pastures, orchards, and woodlots. The setting is pastoral—one you're more likely to share with deer than fellow bipeds.

GET MOVING

Lake Isabella State Park is one of several Washington State Parks properties that were acquired over the years but remain in essence undeveloped. Past state legislatures have not been kind to state park budgets, leaving the agency strapped for funds and relying almost entirely on user fees (Discover Pass and camping fees). Meanwhile, Washington's population continues to burgeon. It would be nice if we could get our state park system up to date to accommodate the growing number

Daffodils blossom around an old farm site at Lake Isabella.

of recreationists—something to ponder as you wander this underutilized property.

There are no signed trails, but it's easy to make your own loops in this property bisected by West Delight Park Road. Start by exploring the northern half of the park. You can walk a faint old farm path across the large rolling field before you get to the old homestead. In spring, a lot of daffodils and other nonnative flowers blossom where farm buildings once stood. There are good views of the lake here too—but no paths down to its shore. The shoreline here is cloaked in thick vegetation, and there are a lot of seeps on the steep slopes leading down to it.

A delightful old farm road leads right (east) here, climbing a forested hill and eventually leading to West Meyenburg Drive. Before reaching that road, turn right on another farm path and enter an old orchard with lake views on the edge of a big, rolling field. From here you can wander the edge of the field back to the trailhead—or veer to the left for a short loop into the forest. The walk around the field is a little less than a mile. You can add an extra half mile or so by following the woods road east of the fields.

South of Delight Park Road is more delightful walking. Access this area by walking across the road from the parking area and picking up an old farm road—or walk east on the field periphery path 0.1 mile, and then take a right onto another old farm road which ducks under Delight Park Road. Both of these approaches meet up in the forest in a little over 0.1 mile. From there, continue walking south another 0.1 mile, coming to a beautiful field. You can follow a path around its periphery for a half mile.

At the field there is another path that leads north, connecting with the western path coming from across the parking area. You can also follow another old farm path south from the field. It comes to a Y junction and then heads left, skirting a fallow upper field being taken over by Scotch broom before coming to a junction in 0.25 mile. Here the path straight continues south, leaving state park property and coming to West Fredson Lane in about 0.3 mile. You want to head right and follow another path north alongside a big wetland, returning to the Y junction in 0.25 mile. Have fun exploring the park!

33 Oakland Bay County Park

DISTANCE:	1.2 miles of trails
ELEVATION GAIN:	Up to 125 feet
HIGH POINT:	100 feet
DIFFICULTY:	Easy
FITNESS:	Walkers, hikers
FAMILY-FRIENDLY:	Yes
DOG-FRIENDLY:	Dogs prohibited
AMENITIES:	Privy, picnic tables, benches
CONTACT/MAPS:	Mason County government; map available online (Parks & Trails homepage)
GPS:	N 47° 14.844", W 123° 01.273"

GETTING THERE

Driving: From Olympia, head north on US Highway 101 to the Olympic Highway (State Route 3) exit in Shelton. Then turn right and follow SR 3 east 9 miles, passing through downtown Shelton. Then turn right onto E. Agate Road and drive 1.5 miles, turning right onto the park access road. (The road is easy to miss. It is 0.5 mile beyond Pioneer Intermediate Middle School and directly across from E. Julian Road.) Now drive this dirt access road 0.4 mile to the trailhead and parking.

Hike through old-growth trees and an old orchard on an old homestead on Oakland Bay. The setting may be old, but the park is new—officially opened in 2013. Explore a salmon-bearing stream and an oyster-rearing tideland. Watch for deer, raccoons, and bald eagles. And check out the historic Malaney-O'Neill House, built in 1892 and originally accessed by boat via the bay. Its size and craftsmanship capture the essence of a prosperous period in the county, when timber was king.

Upper Trail Loop

GET MOVING

From the parking area on a small hill, there are two ways to get down to the historic Malaney-O'Neill House, perched on a small bluff on Oakland Bay. There's the gated service road used by the park steward and for visitors with ADA-plates. You can certainly walk the half mile road—but the Upper Trail is the preferred way to go.

Locate the trailhead next to the privy and begin walking through a grove of big, old bigleaf maples. The well-built trail

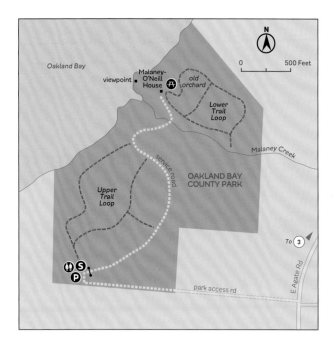

was constructed by a Mason County Youth 4-H forestry crew. This 85-acre park came to be thanks to the Capitol Land Trust and partners who purchased this property for Mason County Parks through a grant from the Recreation and Conservation Office.

In 0.1 mile, come to a junction. Both ways are part of the Upper Trail loop. The way left is slightly longer at about 0.3 mile—while the way right is 0.25 mile. Head left—you'll take the other trail on your return to the trailhead. The trail left descends, passing big cedars and maples. It comes to a bench overlooking the bay before reaching the service road. The return section of the Upper Trail loop can be found just to the right a couple hundred feet up the road. It climbs back up to the loop junction via a ravine.

To get to the Malaney-O'Neill House, turn left and walk the service road 0.15 mile. After crossing Malaney Creek, reach the historic house at an old orchard. Here also find the caretaker's trailer, picnic tables, a privy, and the Lower Trail loop. But before you hike that trail, check out the impressive home, currently being renovated.

The home sits at the edge of the orchard beside some big Doug firs on a small bluff above Oakland Bay. The Malaney-O'Neill House, originally built in 1892 and enlarged a few years later, is one of the best examples of the Carpenter Gothic style in Washington. After admiring this structure, walk the short path behind it to overlook the oyster beds on Oakland Bay. Then go footloose on the Lower Trail loop. Here on a fairly level route, hike through uniform Douglas firs and by a swamp near Malaney Creek. The loop is just shy of a half mile. There's a 0.1-mile connector trail if you want to walk more by doing a figure eight. And there's a short spur to an overlook of the creek. Once you've finished exploring this area, head back up the service road to the Upper Trail and return to the trailhead.

GO FARTHER

Check out the Capitol Land Trust's new Bayshore Preserve across Oakland Bay. There are about 2 miles of trails on this restored parcel, which was once a golf course, along Johns Creek and Oakland Bay. Birdwatching is exceptional. Reach the preserve by traveling east 3.8 miles on SR 3 from Shelton.

Next page: *Dock at Jarrell Cove State Park (Trail 34)*

HARSTINE ISLAND

The largest island in the South Sound, nearly 12,000-acre Harstine Island has fewer than two thousand inhabitants. Connected to the mainland by a bridge over Pickering Passage in 1969, the island until very recently consisted mainly of large tracts of forests owned by timber companies. And while it still remains fairly undeveloped (it has no villages and practically no commercial enterprises), the once-remote island is actively being subdivided for retirees and people seeking second homes. Fortunately, in the last few years, conservation groups have been instrumental in securing for Washington State Parks several large, undeveloped parcels on the island. Among these new park additions are prime, unblemished shorelines offering some of the finest shore walks in Puget Sound.

Controversy surrounds the island's exact spelling. The name has seen multiple spellings, Harstine and Harstene being the most popular. The island was named in 1841 by Lieutenant Wilkes for Lieutenant Henry J. Harstene—who may have spelled his name Harstein. The confusion was finally put to rest in 1997, when the Washington State Legislature settled on Harstine as the island's official name.

34 Jarrell Cove State Park

DISTANCE:	1 mile of trails
ELEVATION GAIN:	80 feet
HIGH POINT:	80 feet
DIFFICULTY:	Easy
FITNESS:	Walkers
FAMILY-FRIENDLY:	Yes
DOG-FRIENDLY:	On-leash
AMENITIES:	Restrooms, water, dock, camping, picnic tables, benches
CONTACT/MAPS:	Washington State Parks; map available online
GPS:	N 47° 16.974", W 122° 53.103"
BEFORE YOU GO:	Discover Pass required

GETTING THERE

Driving: From Olympia, head north on US Highway 101 to the Olympic Highway (State Route 3) exit in Shelton. Then turn right and follow SR 3 east 11 miles, passing through downtown Shelton. Turn right onto E. Pickering Road (signed Harstine Island and Jarrell Cove SP). Follow Pickering for 3.3 miles. Then bear left onto E. Harstine Bridge Road. Drive over the bridge to the island and come to a T junction at 0.6 mile.

Now go left on E. North Island Drive and drive 3 miles to a four-way junction at the island community hall. Continue straight on E. North Island Drive for 0.3 mile and turn left onto E. Wingert Road. Then drive 0.5 mile and turn left onto the state park road. Follow it to the day-use parking area and trailhead.

Primarily a marine camping park, this lovely little state park on the north end of Harstine Island is also accessible by road. Most visitors arrive by boat, and you certainly can too, pulling up to one of the two docks and starting your walk there. But

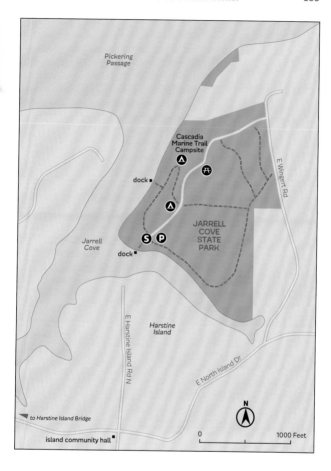

if you arrive by car or bike, start your walk from any of the six short trails taking off from the park road. The park is small—only 43 acres—and the trail system only adds up to about a mile. But it's a pretty and peaceful location. Plan on picnicking afterward—or even spending the night here as a base for exploring the other trail destinations on the island.

Bluff-top trail at Jarrell Cove

GET MOVING

Walk the periphery of the park first by strolling along a bluff above the two slender finger inlets making up Jarrell Cove. The park contains nearly 0.75 mile of shoreline on the cove. Admire the madronas growing along the steep banks of the cove. Definitely hike down to the docks for some great cove views—and the chance to perhaps spot a seal and some marine birds. Then continue walking along the periphery of the park, ambling through mature second-growth firs and thick walls of evergreen huckleberries.

To loop around the entire park, you'll need to walk a little on the quiet park access road. Of course, you can avoid that by doubling back on a couple of the trails leading to the path along the park's periphery. While there is only a mile of trails within the park, you'll be able to walk a little more by creating loops. And if you're camped here, a sunset stroll will be in order—getting you back on the trail for a second hike.

35 Harstine Island State Park

DISTANCE:	3 miles of trails
ELEVATION GAIN:	Up to 200 feet
HIGH POINT:	175 feet
DIFFICULTY:	Easy
FITNESS:	Hikers, runners
FAMILY-FRIENDLY:	Yes
DOG-FRIENDLY:	On-leash
AMENITIES:	Privy, picnic tables, benches
CONTACT/MAPS:	Washington State Parks; no map online
GPS:	N 47° 15.737", W 122° 52.236"
BEFORE YOU GO:	Discover Pass required

GETTING THERE

Driving: From Olympia, head north on US Highway 101 to the Olympic Highway (State Route 3) exit in Shelton. Then turn right and follow SR 3 east 11 miles, passing through downtown Shelton. Turn right onto E. Pickering Road (signed Harstine Island and Jarrell Cove SP). Follow E. Pickering for 3.3 miles. Then bear left onto E. Harstine Bridge Road. Drive over the bridge to the island and come to a T junction at 0.6 mile.

McMicken Island in the distance

Now go left on E. North Island Drive and drive 3 miles to a four-way junction at the island community hall. Turn right onto E. Harstine Island Road North and proceed for 1 mile, turning left onto E. Yates Road. Follow this dirt road (passing a couple of trailheads) for 0.9 mile, and turn right into Harstine Island State Park. Continue 0.2 mile to parking at the main trailhead.

Harstine Island State Park contains more than 300 acres of forest, wetlands, bluffs, and beaches on Case Inlet. Take to 3 miles of trail, exploring thick fir forests, swampy cedar groves, and a lush ravine shaded by towering old-growth. And wander 0.3 mile of cobbled beach, enjoying views of nearby McMicken Island and snowy, showy Mount Rainier in the background. Best of all—this gem of a state park remains off the radar screen of most area hikers. So prepare for some quiet explorations.

GET MOVING

A former Washington DNR property, this forested tract was transferred to Washington State Parks a few decades ago. Most of the old timber was logged, but the forest is recovering nicely, and a small but significant old-growth grove remains on the property. State Parks never got around to developing this property into a full-fledged park. But it's been open to the public for some time, and volunteers have helped expand its trail system. The best thing about this park is that it remains undeveloped—a rarity when so much of Puget Sound has succumbed to wall-to-wall houses.

You definitely want to head to the beach—try to time your visit for a low tide so that the beach is exposed. The two ways to the beach form a loop. The trail on the east end of the parking lot runs along the edge of a 100-foot forested

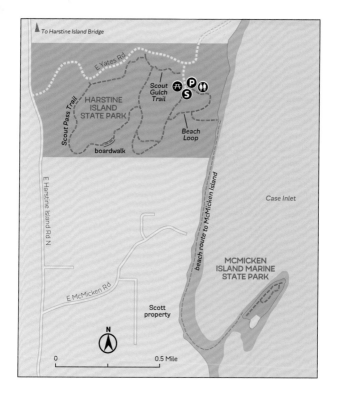

bluff providing glimpses of the remote beach below. It then descends into a cool and dark ravine graced with big cedars and firs, coming to a junction in 0.25 mile. The way right is the continuation of the loop—take that after you've gone left to explore the beach.

Heading left, descend deeper into the ravine. Cross a little creek, and at 0.1 mile from the junction, emerge on the deserted beach. Enjoy the view of McMicken Island and Mount Rainier farther south. Lounge, beachcomb, or hike below the forested bluffs at low tide. The park contains 1600 feet of shoreline.

During minus tides you can walk south on DNR tidelands all the way to a sandbar connecting with McMicken Island Marine State Park. This 11.5-acre park has a half-mile loop in mature timber (watch for poison oak). It's about a 1.2-mile walk along the beach to the island. Respect all private property above the beach that you pass. You'll then enter the McMicken Island Marine State, which incorporates the 112-acre Scott Property on Harstine Island and McMicken Island. Look for the sandbar (consult a tide table so you don't get trapped). Hike the loop trail and explore the shore, but stay off the small parcel of private property on the island's southwest side.

When you're beached out, return to the junction to explore the park's uplands. Continue climbing out of the ravine, passing a few big, ancient cedars spared the axe. In 0.2 mile from the junction, reach another junction. The trail right heads back to the parking lot in 0.2 mile. Go left instead, following a good trail lined with evergreen huckleberries and salal under a canopy of mature second-growth. Pass a trail on your right offering a shortcut. The main route eventually bends around—connecting with the shortcut and coming to a junction in 0.5 mile. From here, you can continue 0.2 mile straight to another junction. Then turn right onto the Scout Gulch Trail, reaching the park road in 0.15 mile. Then walk right 0.1 mile back to the parking lot.

The better choice is to head left on a fairly new trail to a boardwalk through a mossy cedar swamp. At 0.4 mile, this trail comes to a junction with an old logging road. Go right on it, following arrows and coming to the Scout Pass Trail (named for the troops who helped build it—222, 1529, and 9110) in 0.3 mile. Now follow this delightful trail 0.3 mile to a junction. Left goes to a trailhead on East Yates Road. You want to go right, coming to another junction in 0.1 mile. From here turn left on the Scout Gulch Trail, reaching the park road in 0.15 mile. Then walk right 0.1 mile back to the parking lot. Add extra mileage by connecting trails for a good hike or run.

36 Fudge Point State Park

DISTANCE:	3 miles roundtrip with 0.6 mile of beach
ELEVATION GAIN:	175 feet
HIGH POINT:	150 feet
DIFFICULTY:	Easy
FITNESS:	Hikers
FAMILY-FRIENDLY:	Yes
DOG-FRIENDLY:	On-leash
AMENITIES:	None
CONTACT/MAPS:	Washington State Parks; no map online
GPS:	N 47° 13.924", W 122° 52.226"
NOTE:	The park is currently undeveloped but open to the public. Land access is only via a gated logging road. Parking is tight: use the road shoulder; don't block any driveways or access roads. Local resistance to this new park was strong—respect all private property and be on your absolute best behavior.

GETTING THERE

Driving: From Olympia, head north on US Highway 101 to the Olympic Highway (State Route 3) exit in Shelton. Then turn right and follow SR 3 east 11 miles, passing through downtown Shelton. Turn right onto E. Pickering Road (signed Harstine Island and Jarrell Cove SP). Follow Pickering for 3.3 miles. Then bear left onto E. Harstine Bridge Road. Drive over the bridge to the island and come to a T junction at 0.6 mile. Turn right onto E. South Island Drive and continue for 3.3 miles to a junction. Now go left on E. Harstine Island Road North for 0.2 mile. Turn right on E. Ballow Road and drive 0.8 mile to where the road makes a sharp bend left. Park here (see note above).

Walk a logging road to a 136-acre parcel of pure natural splendor. The new Fudge Point State Park contains one of the wildest and best beaches remaining in the South Sound. Walk 3200 feet (a full kilometer) of wide sandy beach, passing productive tidelands and a wildlife-rich marsh and small delta. Enjoy sweeping views of Case Inlet, from Herron Island and the Key Peninsula to mighty Mount Rainier hovering over

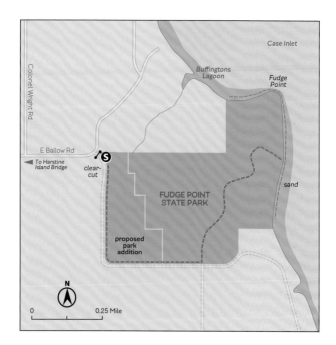

maritime mist. Fudge Point is one of the sweetest places on Puget Sound. And you'll savor your visits here for a long time.

GET MOVING

Washington State Parks touts Fudge Point as having the potential to be one of Washington's greatest state parks. It's quite remarkable that a large, pristine stretch of South Sound shoreline was able to remain undeveloped and unblemished for this long. In 2013, with help from The Trust for Public Land, State Parks was able to purchase 60 acres of land consisting of 3200 feet of shoreline at Fudge Point. The following year, with the help of the Washington Wildlife and Recreation Coalition, State Parks purchased 76 acres of adjacent uplands. The state is currently trying to buy another adjoining 47 acres. The plan is to keep the shoreline intact, adding just a few trails while providing a small area for parking, day use, and camping. It may be some time before all of this happens. But you don't need to wait to experience this park—and its wide and wild sandy beach.

Where the road bends near a recent clear-cut, find two dirt roads. You want to walk on the gated one, east of the bend. It immediately turns south and skirts a recent clear-cut. The land on the left is the parcel State Parks is currently trying to purchase. Walk the near-level road. In 0.4 mile, it makes a ninety-degree turn left. Continue walking, coming to a four-way road junction at 0.8 mile. The roads right and straight lead to private lots and homes. The one left is the one you want. Take it and immediately be greeted by a sign indicating you are entering state park land. Rejoice—this won't get subdivided! Now walk this nice country road lined with foxglove and shaded by alders and maples, and slowly descend toward the shore. At 1.5 miles, reach the beach. Now let the magic begin.

Walk north 0.25 mile on a wide, sandy, and small-cobbled beach rounding Fudge Point. The park boundary is at the

Deserted sandy beach at Fudge Point

small delta draining an upland marsh. Sit here (but don't go into the marsh) for a while and watch for all kinds of avian and mammalian activity. The tideland in front of you (below mean low tide) is home to a geoduck farm owned by Taylor Shellfish. There are usually workers out and about tending the farm.

Now retrace your steps, rounding Fudge Point once more. The small island to your east is privately owned Herron Island, accessed by private ferry from the Key Peninsula. Keep walking south, now looking down Case Inlet to the Nisqually Reach and up to majestic Mount Rainier. It is one of the prettiest maritime scenes in the South Sound. At 0.6 mile from your turnaround (0.35 mile from the trail), you'll come to a survey post marking the park's southern boundary. Turn around and find yourself a great place to lounge for a while before making the 1.5-mile hike back to your car. Be appreciative of this special property—and thankful to the government officials and private conservation interests that made it happen. And be sure to support your parks and these organizations so they can maintain these beautiful properties and acquire more.

RESOURCES

CONTACTS

Evergreen State College
(360) 867-6000
http://evergreen.edu/tour/trailmaps.htm

Lacey
William Ives Trail
www.ci.lacey.wa.us

Woodland Creek Community Park
www.ci.lacey.wa.us

Mason County Parks and Recreation
Goldsborough Creek Trail
www.co.mason.wa.us/forms/parks/trails_map.pdf

Huff N Puff Trail
www.co.mason.wa.us/forms/parks/trails_map.pdf
(Also see entry under Shelton Metropolitan Park District)

Oakland Bay County Park
www.co.mason.wa.us/forms/parks/oakland_bay_trails_and
_walking_map.pdf

Olympia Metropolitan Parks District
Priest Point
http://olympiawa.gov/community/parks/parks-and-trails
/priest-point-park.aspx

Watershed Park
http://olympiawa.gov/community/parks/parks-and-trails
/watershed-park.aspx

Olympia Tumwater Foundation
Tumwater Falls
www.olytumfoundation.org

Shelton Metropolitan Park District
Huff N Puff Trail
www.ci.shelton.wa.us/departments/parks_and_recreation
/index.php
(Also see entry under Mason County Parks and Recreation)

Thurston County Parks and Recreation
Burfoot County Park
www.co.thurston.wa.us/parks/parks-burfoot.htm

Chehalis Western Trail
www.co.thurston.wa.us/parks/trails-chehalis-western.htm

Frye Cove County Park
www.co.thurston.wa.us/parks/parks-fryecove.htm

Yelm–Tenino Trail
www.co.thurston.wa.us/parks/trails-yelm-tenino.htm

Tumwater Parks and Recreation
Pioneer Park
www.ci.tumwater.wa.us/Home/Components
/FacilityDirectory/FacilityDirectory/22/479

US Fish and Wildlife Service
Billy Frank Jr. Nisqually National Wildlife Refuge
www.fws.gov/refuge/billy_frank_jr_nisqually

Washington Department of Fish and Wildlife
(360) 249-4628
Scatter Creek Wildlife Area
Coast Region 6 (Montesano)
http://wdfw.wa.gov

Washington Department of Natural Resources
Southwest Puget Sound Regional Office DNR
(360) 825-1631

Capitol State Forest
www.dnr.wa.gov/Capitol

Mima Mounds Natural Area Preserve
www.dnr.wa.gov/MimaMounds

Woodard Bay Natural Resources Conservation Area
www.dnr.wa.gov/WoodardBay

Washington Department of Transportation
www.wsdot.wa.gov

Washington Department of Enterprise Services
Capitol Lake Parks and Trails
http://des.wa.gov/services/facilities/CapitolCampus/Parks
/Pages/Trails.aspx

Washington State Parks
http://parks.state.wa.us
Parks information center: (360) 902-8844
Contact them for information about Fudge Point, Harstine Island, and Lake Isabella.

Jarrell Cove State Park
(360) 426-9226
http://parks.state.wa.us/523/Jarrell-Cove

Lake Isabella State Park
Map: www.co.mason.wa.us/forms/parks/trails_map.pdf

Millersylvania State Park
(360) 753-1519
http://parks.state.wa.us/546/Millersylvania

Tolmie State Park
(360) 456-6464
http://parks.state.wa.us/297/Tolmie

TRAIL AND CONSERVATION ORGANIZATIONS

Capitol Land Trust
https://capitollandtrust.org

Center for Natural Lands Management
http://cnlm.org

Creekside Conservancy
http://creeksideconservancy.org

Forterra
http://forterra.org

Friends of Capitol Forest
www.friendsofcapitolforest.org

The Mountaineers
www.mountaineers.org

The Nature Conservancy
www.nature.org

Nisqually Land Trust
http://nisquallylandtrust.org

Olympia Mountaineers
www.olympiamountaineers.org

Washington Nature Conservancy
www.nature.org/ourinitiatives/regions/northamerica
/unitedstates/washington

Washington State Parks Foundation
http://wspf.org

Washington Trails Association
www.wta.org

Washington Wildlife and Recreation Coalition
www.wildliferecreation.org

Woodland Trail Greenway Association
http://wtga.org

RUNNING CLUBS AND ORGANIZED RUNS, HIKES, AND WALKS IN AND AROUND OLYMPIA

Club Oly Road Runners

An affiliate member of Road Runners Club of America and the Pacific Northwest Association of USA Track & Field, this club sponsors group runs, a cross-country series, and a handful of races.
www.clubolyrunning.com

Guerilla Running Racing Club

An Olympia-based running club that sponsors training groups, a racing team, and several organized races, including the Mountain Marathon and Hillbilly Half Marathon held at Capitol State Forest.
www.guerillarunning.com

The Mountaineers

A Seattle-based outdoors club that also has an Olympia branch. They are involved with local conservation issues and also coordinate group outdoor activities.
www.mountaineers.org

Olympia Lakefair Run

A popular annual race—the 8K event is among one of the longest continuously held running races in Washington. It and the 3K utilize the Capitol Lake Trail. The newer half marathon includes stretches on the Chehalis Western and Woodland trails.
www.ontherunevents.com/lakefair

Oly Trail Runners

An Olympia-based trail running club that also sponsors a series of trail races at Capitol State Forest known as the Capitol Peak Ultras.
www.olytrailrunners.com/capitol-peak-ultras

South Sound Running

A running specialty store in Tumwater that sponsors training groups.
www.southsoundrunning.com

ACKNOWLEDGMENTS

Researching and writing *Urban Trails: Olympia* was fun, gratifying, and a lot of hard work. I couldn't have finished this project without the help and support of the following people. A huge thank you to all the great people at Mountaineers Books, especially publisher, Helen Cherullo, editor-in-chief, Kate Rogers, and project manager Laura Shauger.

A big thank you to my editor, Emily Barnes, for her attention to detail and thoughtful suggestions helping to make this book a finer volume. I also want to thank my wife, Heather, and son, Giovanni, for accompanying me on many of the trails in this book. A big thanks too to Jay Thompson, Maxine Dunkelman, and Ray Philen for providing excellent trail company. And I thank God for watching over me and keeping me safe and healthy while I hiked and ran all over Olympia and its environs!

Porter Trail (Trail 25), Capitol State Forest

INDEX

ABOUT THE
AUTHOR

Craig Romano grew up in rural New Hampshire where he fell in love with the natural world. He moved to Washington in 1989 and has since hiked more than 30,000 miles in the Evergreen State. An avid runner as well, Craig has run more than thirty marathons and ultra runs, including the Boston Marathon and the White River 50-Mile Endurance Run.

An award-winning author and co-author of more than twenty-five books, Craig also writes for numerous publications, tourism websites, and Hikeoftheweek.com. His book *Columbia Highlands: Exploring Washington's Last Frontier* was recognized in 2010 by Washington Secretary of State Sam Reed and State Librarian Jan Walsh as a "Washington Reads" book for its contribution to the state's cultural heritage.

When not hiking, running, and writing, Craig can be found napping with his wife, Heather, son, Giovanni, and Maine coon cat, Beau, at his home in Skagit County. Visit him at http://CraigRomano.com and on Facebook at "Craig Romano Guidebook Author."